W9-ATU-083

Gardening
with the Goddess

Creating Gardens
of Spirit and Magick

Gardening
with the Goddess

Creating Gardens
of Spirit and Magick

By
Patricia Telesco

NEW PAGE BOOKS
A division of The Career Press, Inc.
Franklin Lakes, NJ

Copyright © 2001 by Patricia Telesco

All rights reserved under the Pan-American and International Copyright Conventions. This book may not be reproduced, in whole or in part, in any form or by any means electronic or mechanical, including photocopying, recording, or by any information storage and retrieval system now known or hereafter invented, without written permission from the publisher, The Career Press.

Gardening With the Goddess
Cover design by Cheryl Finbow
Edited and typeset by Jodi L. Brandon
Printed in the U.S.A. by Book-mart Press

To order this title, please call toll-free 1-800-CAREER-1 (NJ and Canada: 201-848-0310) to order using VISA or MasterCard, or for further information on books from Career Press.

The Career Press, Inc., 3 Tice Road, PO Box 687, Franklin Lakes, NJ 07417
www.careerpress.com
www.newpagebooks.com

Library of Congress Cataloging-in-Publication Data

Telesco, Patricia, 1960-
    Gardening with the Goddess : how to create gardens of spirit and magick / by Patricia Telesco.
        p. cm.
    Includes bibliographical references and index.
    ISBN 1-56414-553-0 (pbk.)
    1. Gardening—Miscellanea. 2. Goddess religion. 3. Magic. I. Title.

    BF1623.G37 .T45 2001
    635—dc21   00-065387

Dedication

For the broad-based Neo-Pagan community, whose diversity is as wonderful and colorful as the flowers of the Earth. Gentle Winds and Sweet Waters be yours!

Contents

Introduction

> If you have a garden and a library,
> you have everything you need.
> —*Marcus Tullius Cicero*

The wonder and adoration humans hold for natural things is nearly unquenchable. And who can really blame us? When we look at the earth with appreciative eyes, we're drawn in by its beauty, diversity, and many wonders. That's probably the reason why gardening is the most popular hobby in North America. People garden in order to enjoy the earth's loveliness and variety on an intimate level—and hopefully to dig up the answers to a few ageless riddles in the process!

Think of it this way: We live in right-brain, technological times filled with pollution, noise, metal, and an ever-increasing sense of impersonalization. Everything is "by the numbers." However, the ancient art of gardening offers us a chance to change the way we cope with this reality and maybe even shake it up a bit! Whether you live in an apartment or a home, puttering with soil and seed, even just a little, is very healthy for one's mind and spirit. It provides a few moments of peace and a chance to ground ourselves in the Mother once more. Perhaps more importantly, gardening offers us an opportunity to simply be, without anyone or anything else dictating that sense of being.

An additional benefit of gardening is that it becomes a classroom. Here we learn directly from nature's textbook. Our ancestors felt strongly that working the land also worked the soul. Even one hundred years ago people were still talking about how Nature reflected God and was a means to better understanding that great mystery (of who or what God is). The more we lost sight of the human-nature-creator trinity, the more we abused our world and lost an appreciation for its lessons and the further we removed ourselves from important spiritual truths. A century later, we have begun to see how destructive that trend in humankind was becoming, for both the Earth and its inhabitants.

So how do we go about bringing the Goddess and our gardening back together? A good part of this question is answered when we realize that the two were never really apart. Just because humans lose sight of a connection doesn't mean the Goddess does likewise! The Goddess is already firmly rooted in our gardens.

Many of the world's myths depict the Goddess at the Creatrix, and frequently Her names magnify one or more of Nature's realms. For example, in Roman tradition Flora embodies all forms of blossoming and fertility. (We continue to use the word *flora* today to describe blossoming things.) In Canaanite tradition, Asherah's name means "upright" even as the trees that were thought to contain her energy. Greek tradition has Demeter (the "Earth Mother") as the goddess of Earth, groves, and all growing things.

In fact, one would be hard-pressed to find any culture that didn't include the Goddess interacting with, protecting, facilitating, and monitoring nature on some level in the myths and lore of its people. The power of these myths should not be underestimated, as they still affect the way we think and communicate. After all, we still use the phrases "Mother Nature" and "Mother Earth" in conversation regularly. This indicates that the connection between Earth and the Goddess remains very powerful—even if we don't always recognize that connection. Part of the goal of *Gardening with the Goddess* is to begin conscientiously re-establishing that awareness, our ties to this planet, and relationship with the ever-welcoming energy of the Goddess.

Building on that foundation, *Gardening with the Goddess* looks at the way we garden in a slightly different way: by bringing common metaphysical processes into our efforts, such as blessing the soil, energizing it with spellcraft, following the moon's cycles, using crystals to enhance plant growth, and returning to natural methods of working the land. It is fairly safe to say that an organic gardener is also a good steward of the planet, and a spiritually minded organic gardener is a good co-creator with the Goddess! These ideas will be covered in detail in Part 1: Goddess-Centered Thinking.

With the basic methods and ideology out of the way, the next logical step is creating some gardens. In Part 2: Goddess Gardens, I explore various theme gardens (both indoors and out). Here you'll discover a magickal garden dedicated to Hecate, the patroness of witches, a fairy garden dedicated to Dana, the mother of the Fey, and even a zen-styled rock and sand garden that honors the spirit of mental and spiritual liberation.

And what exactly can you do with all these gardens? Quite a bit. They can become sacred spaces where you perform rituals and spells, akin to a natural temple. Or, you can harvest magickally empowered flowers, fruits, herbs, and vegetables from here for use at home and in Circle. And, of course, you could simply sit here, meditate, and enjoy the view!

Because there are literally thousands of goddesses depicted in the world's mythology, I can only cover a few here. This sampling should nonetheless inspire your imagination and help you find personal ways to honor the Goddess in your garden, no matter by what name you call Her! No matter the name, however, I hope that you find you enjoy gardening more by the end of this book, and appreciate the magick of those moments, both subtle and sublime.

With a little thoughtfulness and old-fashioned elbow grease, gardening and landscaping have the capacity to become a kind of spiritual therapy. Here, you consult with Nature, lay the worries of the day and other tensions neatly at the feet of the Mother, and then grow something beautiful in their place: a renewed sense of self, the planet, and Spirit.

Part 1:
Goddess-Centered
Thinking

There's music in the sighing of a reed;
there's music in the gushing of a rill;
there's music in all things,
if men had ears.

—Lord Byron

As you've probably already gathered, I'm an avid gardener. In fact, my husband worries that some day he'll come home to find the entire lawn landscaped. (Truth be told, he just might!) How exactly did I get so enamored with playing in the dirt?

Thinking back on my childhood I remember my neighbor having a huge garden from which she picked, cooked, and often canned fresh goods that were simply delicious. I also remember that whenever I wanted time to myself I'd go to Nature's supermarket and forage for berries in the nearby woods. There I would wander around skipping rocks and singing to the trees.

Although these memories got lost for a while amid normal teenage angst and harried college activity, they returned after I gave birth to my first child. I wanted him to be able to savor the fresh taste of green beans and peas and to know the wonder of watching things that you've planted and tended with love grow.

Sure, I made some mistakes in my first garden. Some of the things I started from seed way too late, others I overwatered, and others still were simply ill-suited to poorly drained city soil. Even so, we had wonderful tomatoes, onions, and a few carrots that year. To this day, I don't think anything has tasted quite so good as that first ripe cherry tomato. I was hooked.

I also became involved with pleasure herbalism—making oils, soaps, incense, brews, and the like. This hobby provided another list of things to try growing in my garden! Herbs also proved to have little idiosyncracies that I had to learn about by trial and error. For example, never grow mint unless you want *a lot* of it... and I do mean tons! It grows like crazy, often taking over the whole garden, and is very hard to weed out because of its root systems. Like my first attempt with vegetables, though, there was so much fun in the discovery process that the mistakes seemed small by comparison.

This book is the result of my adventures in gardening and landscaping, combined with my love of the Goddess and magickal living. It includes my failures and successes in the hopes that you can benefit from both. In this section in particular we'll look at some of the mundane considerations for gardening, as well as some of the most common metaphysical compliments that help bring the Goddess more directly into your handiwork.

Goddess Who?

Who comprehends her? With whom can one
consult concerning this great goddess?
—*Ludwig van Beethoven*

The idea of Goddess spirituality is fairly new to a lot of people, so I'd like to share a brief glimpse of what this approach to life is all about. Without a foundation in this epistemology, it's hard to understand and apply the rest of this book effectively. In particular, this segue will be helpful to readers who have never considered the Goddess as a life partner (or never even thought about the feminine Divine at all).

If we turn back the pages of time and look at early humankind, we find dozens of images of a female Creatrix. Because it is the women of our species who produce children, it makes sense that at least some of our ancestors perceived the original Sacred Parent as female. The names these goddesses bore varied from culture to culture and era to era, as did many of their attributes. Some goddesses governed the moon, others the land, others still human fertility and matters of the heart. In this manner, early people created an array of goddess mythos that could easily be applied to daily life and needs. It is in this mythos that Goddess spirituality finds its roots.

Here, suddenly...and almost foreignly to our modern minds, God is a woman. She is full-breasted, pregnant, and ever-fertile. She is the First Source, providing life and nourishment to all living things. She can be fiercely protective, impassioned, or compassionate, depending on the situation. She *is* all, above all, below all, and within all. She is past, present, future, and eternal. She is as she is.

That said, Goddess spirituality does not limit the image of the Divine to being only female. Just like the yin-yang image, there is balance in all spiritual things. The reason for stressing the female portion of the Divine has come about due to two millennia of male dominance in society and in many religions. This left women without strong sacred role models. It also left men without a guideline for integrating various traits that are traditionally considered "feminine" in alignment (such as sensitivity and nurturing).

In effect, the Goddess movement helps swing the pendulum in the other direction and offers us a chance to re-establish symmetry. It also provides a great intuitive balance to our very scientifically oriented world. Does this mean you can't honor the God in your garden? Of course not! It simply means that, in this book at least, we will be looking to various goddesses to guide, energize, and bless our proverbial green thumbs! There is absolutely no reason not to tweak the ideas presented here for masculine images of the Divine if you so choose—or better still, create matching god and goddess gardens!

Here is a brief list of some global goddesses and the plants they held sacred. This will be particularly useful in creating goddess-themed gardens for divine figures not covered in this book:

Goddess Sacred Plants

Aphrodite	Apple, beet, marjoram, myrtle, rose
Artemis	Daisy, willow
Athena	Mulberry, oak
Bast	Catnip
Ceres	Bay
Bon Dea	Myrtle
Brigit	Blackberry
Ceres	Poppy
Cybele	Ivy, pine
Danu	Meadowsweet
Demeter	Bean, corn, poppy, rose, sunflower
Diana	Apple, vervain, willow
Flora	Hawthorn
Freya	Daisy, primrose, strawberry
Gaia	Fruit (all)
Hecate	Dandelion, garlic, lavender, mint
Hera	Apple, heather, iris
Io	Violet
Isis	Heather, narcissus, rose
Iznagi	Grape, peach
Juno	Heather, lily
Kwan Yin	Lily
Lilith	Tarragon
Min	Lettuce
Persephone	Parsley
Rhea	Oak, pine

Utto	Cucumber
Venus	Apple, cinnamon, marjoram, parsley, violet

For those of you who may not consider yourself terribly religious or deity-oriented, that need not limit your use of this book. You can, instead, think of Goddess spirituality as a philosophy. This approach to life advocates the following:

♦ Earth-responsible living (global awareness).
♦ Intuitive, proactive approaches to problem-solving.
♦ Progressive and creative spiritual pursuits.
♦ An awareness of the sacredness and magick in all things.
♦ A personal vision and self-awareness.
♦ Thinking and living "out of the box."

In this case, rather than using the specific names of the goddesses, simply consider each as a symbol of a vibration to which you're attuning the plants in your garden. Effectively, this attracts that specific energy into your greenery and, indeed, helps you cultivate that attribute or energy in your life!

Practical and Metaphysical Considerations

Gardening requires a lot of water—most of it
in the form of perspiration.
—*Lou Erickson*

The Goddess has always been a very practical woman. She understands all too well that not all of us have a lot of free time, abundant open spaces, a good source of gardening know-how and tools, or even good nurseries/seed outlets from which to cultivate our spiritual gardens. She also knows that in order for any garden to be successful, we have to first consider all of these issues as they may affect our daily lives.

I'm not going to fib and say that gardens don't take some time in order to achieve success. The smaller the effort, the less time involved. Be forewarned that even a small garden can become quite addicting, and you may find yourself adding more, or spending more time working it, than you expected initially.

To be honest, starting out small has numerous advantages. You can really get to know a few plant types, what they like, what they don't like, and how to handle their needs. You can also direct more energy into them because you're focusing on a confined space. Additionally, each type of greenery has magickal associations ascribed to it, so you can augment those associations through that focus if you choose.

For those of you with little space, starting small is a necessity. (Because more and more of us live in urban environments with limited lawns, I include lots of hints for adjusting your gardening efforts to the space available.) Trust me when I say that there's a lot you can do with porch pots and window boxes, especially if you like tomatoes, flowers, and herbs.

Both small and large gardens require a few good tools, many of which you may be able to make out of kitchen implements or buy inexpensively at secondhand and discount stores. There are also some niceties that you may find you want as you garden more. The basics are listed here. (More specific items are listed in Part II as they pertain to unique garden efforts.)

Space

Whether it's a patch of yard or several window boxes and planters, you need room within which your plants can grow. If this space is within the line of sight, all the better. Seeing the garden regularly reminds you to tend it and send good energy its way on a regular basis.

Soil

You can add some potting soil or topsoil, compost, or other fertilizers to yard dirt if it's leached of nutrients (see "Gaia's Built-in Helpers" later this chapter for ideas). Note: Always read up on the kind of soil your plants like. Some want rocky foundations for drainage, others like sand, others like loam. The better you prepare your soil to the plants chosen, the greater success you will have.

Hand Tools

A trowel, spade, or a sturdy spoon works for digging up small efforts. A good shovel will be necessary for yard work, and a sturdy garden rake is very helpful for landscaping and larger outdoor efforts. (Though not tools per se, garden gloves and knee pads save a lot of wear and tear on your hands and clothes, respectively.)

Fencing

If you need to keep pets or children out of a garden (or if your yard is accessible to wandering animals), fencing is well worth considering. Fencing is sometimes necessary for certain types of climbing greenery, such as ivy and honeysuckle.

Seeds, Seedlings, or Plants

Take your time and shop around for good sources. You want good quality young plants to achieve the best quality gardens. (Although an accomplished gardener *can* often nurse sickly plants back to health, it takes a lot of extra time and effort.)

I suggest garden outlets (and nurserymen) in your area, where you can go and feel out the plants (not to mention survey their physical condition and the condition of the outlet), as a good source. Look for stores where the plants are set up in an orderly fashion, where the salespeople are knowledgeable, and where the plants look well-tended. A lot of wilted, browning, or pale plants are not signs of a good nursery.

Avoid Internet purchases unless you know the source (or can confirm its quality). Remember that you won't see these plants in person until after they're paid for. That caution aside, I have had reasonable success getting plants at online auction houses from established buyers.

Decorative Touches

I'm one of those people who has to tweak everything, including Nature. Mind you, decorative touches can be very utilitarian, such as a rabbit that disguises a watering device, a fountain to attract birds or butterflies, or a trellis for climbing flowers and vegetables. On the other hand, these touches can be purely whimsical, such as statuary and special edging that make the whole garden "pop."

How much or little embellishing you do is completely up to you, but make sure these additions match the goddess theme you're trying to create. For example, when doing an Athenic garden, it makes sense to look into a statue of Athena as a centerpiece or accent point. Similarly, in a garden for Pax, the goddess of peace, it would be nice to have white stones and large pieces of amethyst to accent that harmonious energy.

Another nice touch that honors your land is to keep any sizable stones you dig up and use them as borders, plant markers, or accent pieces. Wash these off and allow your intuition to guide you in their placement. If you think for a moment of large stone circles, such as Stonehenge and Callanish, this type of rock placement is quite traditional at sacred sites, which is what your garden is becoming. You're just doing it on a smaller scale.

Resource Information

I strongly recommend getting at least two good garden encyclopedias or magazine subscriptions that cover the types of plants with which you want to work. Alternatively, take a little time surfing the net for garden-oriented sites. Don't be surprised to discover literally thousands of sites dedicated to gardening. Compare and contrast the ideas they offer. It may take a little diligence to weed through them, but I promise you'll pull up at least a handful that you'll want to return to again and again. Bookmark them!

There are some wonderful "real life" resources out there, too, such as home and garden shows, garden clubs, arborariums, greenhouses, and so forth. Some of these resources offer free information for those baffling garden questions; others have some available at very low costs (in some cases, the entry fee to the home show).

No matter your tact, having good resources will make your gardening efforts much more pleasant from the get-go because you can benefit from other people's mistakes and triumphs.

Gaia's Built-in Helpers

A prudent man does not make the goat his gardener.
—*Hungarian Proverb*

If you talk to people living a metaphysical lifestyle, most will advocate natural foods and flowers rather than those that are treated. Chemicals don't necessarily mix well with magick. For one, we cannot be completely certain what type of energies these things bear when we blend them into our mixes. For another, anything that's consumed, buried, burned, or scattered to the winds will carry those chemicals back to the planet, which isn't really an Earth-friendly approach!

Unfortunately, the soil in a lot of people's yards isn't always the best, and insects are certainly part of nature, even if we might wish otherwise. Rather than simply reach for an over-the-counter preparation that may not be good for the planet or for spiritual pursuits, however, I feel it's important to consider alternatives. Many of these alternatives come to us from our ancestors who didn't have the advantage of man-made pest deterrents.

Companion Planting

Thankfully our ancestors left us a wealth of knowledge about Nature's little helpers: plants that help other plants grow, plants that deter specific types of bugs, and even plants that make for tastier vegetables! This approach is known as companion planting.

Let's first look at plants that enhance flavor. According to tradition one should plant basil with tomatoes, dill with cabbage, mustard with beans, and dandelion with apples. On the other hand, it's not recommended that sage and onion be grown in the same garden, nor cabbage and grapes. Similarly don't put blackberries, lilac, azalea, or rhododendrons anywhere near black walnut trees, anise near carrots, chives near peas, dill near tomatoes, garlic near beans, marigolds near beans, or mustard near turnips. Although this information hasn't been "proven," old-time gardeners swear by it!

Next, consider the plants that are said to help other plants grow more fully and abundantly. Use this list in considering the way you plan the layout of your garden. Pair:

- Bean with mustard or rosemary.
- Carrot with chives or sage.
- Coriander with anise.
- Cucumber with chamomile.
- Lettuce with chrysanthemum.
- Marigold with tomato or rose.
- Onion with dill.
- Pepper with basil.
- Potato with horseradish or thyme.
- Rose with garlic or onion.
- Strawberry with onion or sage.
- Tomato with mint.
- Vegetables (general) with tarragon.

If you decide to try companion planting, you can approach it several ways. The first is to simply plant one tomato plant followed by a mint plant in a row, and then repeat. The second approach is to have one whole row of tomatoes with a row of mint adjacent. (With this particular combination, I'd recommend the second approach because of mint's propensity to send out abundant root systems and take over space.) The third approach is to plant decoratively, such as two or three tomato plants surrounded in a circle of mint, which is quite pleasing to the eye and still serves the enrichment function. This last option is particularly nice for goddess gardens where one is trying to build multisensual energy that reaches out to the mind and spirit at the same time.

Bug Repellents

Similar to the way they pair plants so that they grow better, old-time gardeners also used various bits of greenery to deter bugs. Here's a list of some of the plants used to keep specific insects away from the garden:

Ant	Mint, tansy
Aphids	Garlic
Asparagus beetle	Basil, tomato
Beetle	Parsley
Cabbage butterfly	Southernwood
Carrot fly	Leek, rosemary, sage
Flea beetle	Sage, tobacco, thyme
Japanese beetle	Chive, garlic
Nematode	Marigold
Potato beetle	Tansy, catnip, nasturtium, marigold
Peach aphid	Catnip
Slug	Wormwood
Squash bug	Tansy
Whitefly	Nasturtium

Note that some items even deter mice, rabbits, or moles, such as wormwood, garlic or marigold, and narcissus respectively.

If you're looking at this list and thinking it's impossible to plant everything necessary to keep your garden insect-free, there's an alternative. Get some fresh leaves and flowers from tomatoes, sage, wormwood, marigolds, and other pest repellents and boil them in water. The stronger this mixture is, the better. (Just cover the plants with water and simmer until it makes a strong tea.) Sprinkle this on your garden after every rain. The aromatics may not be as strong as having fresh-growing items, but it saves space and provides some ongoing protection.

Natural Fertilizers

One of the best natural fertilizers can be made by filling a household bucket with nettles, dandelions, valerian, yarrow, chamomile, and oak bark. Cover this with water and leave it in the sun for three weeks. Water your plants with this once a week. The residuals from this fertilizing tea can be easily turned into compost.

Speaking of compost, this is an excellent way to recycle and enrich your soil at the same time. Coffee grounds, hair, vegetable ends and pieces, grass clippings, peanut shells, sawdust, egg shells, and fish are all compostable. Do, however, check local regulations about what type of container you need for compost so that you don't get fined or attract rodents.

Finally, another way to improve the yield in your garden is to attract "good" bugs (those that pollinate your plants). Queen Anne's lace, flowering carrot, and fennel encourage these visitors.

For those of you who don't have time to make your own fertilizers and repellents, many garden and nursery outlets now offer the organic alternatives. They tend to cost a little more, but they are certainly more reflective of everything we're trying to honor and achieve in our goddess gardens. Two other alternatives exist too: mulch and weed block.

Mulch comes in a variety of types, including cedar, pine, wormwood, and hardwood. Mulch gives a garden a nice, finished look. Some kinds of mulch deter insects (other than wood ants), and all deter weed growth. Better still, mulch doesn't hurt the soil in the least. You can simply turn it into the earth at the end of the season.

Weed block is a type of cloth that blocks sunlight but allows water through. Thus the soil continues to receive moisture but any weeds beneath will not grow from the lack of sun. Typically something is placed on top of the weed block once it's laid around your plants, such as mulch or landscaping stone.

I do not recommend using stone over weed block unless the plants are a fairly permanent choice, because moving the stone to replace plants is difficult and laborious. Additionally, white stone (which is the least expensive and most common) shows stains easily and looks dingy after a while. If you decide on stone, go with something that's got a variety of colors or begins with a brown tone for longer-lasting visual appeal.

Gardening and the Seasons

The seed waits for its garden or ground
where it will be sown.
—*Zulu Proverb*

Few of us live close to the land any more. We get busy and before we know it entire years have passed by with little notice of the changing seasons and the Earth's cycles. To be a successful magickal gardener, however, you have to determine here and now to forestall this trend. Quite simply stated, it's nearly impossible to work with Earth's elements and energies when you're not paying attention to the Earth!

This doesn't mean buying a house in the country and returning to an agrarian lifestyle. In fact, re-attuning yourself to natural cycles requires very few changes other than the way you look at the world (and how you interpret what you see).

For example, consider the differences in light entering your home first thing in the morning during Spring and Summer versus Fall and Winter. How does that brightness change the way you feel? Extending that idea, how does the sun's brightness change the way everything outside looks and feels? Doesn't everything seem more alive and vibrant when the sun is shining? Don't you often feel similarly revitalized when a lovely ray of sunlight greets the breakfast table? This very simple observation is an excellent example of how to begin reconnecting with nature in very substantive ways.

In particular the magickal gardener wants to be sensitive to weather changes and how these shifts affect plants and the energy they bear. For example, garlic is traditionally considered a Fire herb because of its pungent aroma and strong flavor. But what about garlic that's been grown in a particularly rainy season? Might that garlic not be a little less Fire-oriented, and even perhaps blend the energies of Water and Fire together? Similarly, if you harvest garlic during a wind storm, could that timing bring the Element of Air into play? Sure it could. It's this kind of creative, intuitive insight that goddess gardening advocates.

The goddess-centered gardener also wants to be able to recognize Earth's signals so that he or she can weed, plant, water, fertilize, and sow more effectively. You can use the growing guide that follows here as a "starter," but remember that gardening isn't a perfect art. We can't simply write up a standardized how-to that will suit every location, soil type, shifts in animal and insect habitats, and variations in the climate. By attuning yourself to your area and nature's harbingers from that area, you will become a proverbial "green thumb" (often befuddling neighbors and friends by growing things when everyone else is experiencing failure).

Abbreviated Growing Guide

- Alfalfa prefers damp, rich soil with sun/shade mix.
- Aloe grows in well-drained soil with a mingling of light and shade.
- Anise grows best in hilly areas with good drainage and sunlight.
- Asparagus prefers loamy soil laden with clay in partial sunlight.
- Basil requires rich soil and plenty of sun. Transplant it only after the risk of frost passes.
- Bay requires well-drained soil and partial sun. Sow from cuttings.
- Bayberry thrives with rhododendrons nearby, especially in sandy soil.
- Beans, though fairly hearty, cannot be planted when there's a risk of below-the-soil-line frost.
- Cabbage requires fertile soil, plenty of sun, and regular watering to keep the roots damp.
- Carnation likes sandy soil and partial sun.
- Carrot prefers well-aerated soil with sun/shade mixture.
- Celery thrives best in damp or wet soil.
- Chamomile prefers dry or sandy soil with plentiful sun.
- Chive prefers rich soil with good drainage in full sun.
- Chrysanthemum grows well in open spaces, especially when watered bi-weekly.
- Daisy enjoys moist soil and requires a bed of straw for winter.
- Dill likes moist, good soil with plentiful sun.

- Fennel requires average soil with good drainage. Full sunlight is recommended.
- Ginger requires good soil with good drainage and some shade.
- Horseradish needs good, moist soil with plentiful sun.
- Jasmine needs a warm environment and loam-rich soil.
- Lavender likes well-aerated and drained soil with plentiful sunlight and a bit of lime.
- Lilac needs soil high in acid and plentiful space.
- Magnolia fares best in warm climates where the soil is rich but the sunlight is not direct.
- Marigold tolerates a lot of conditions, as long as it's planted after the threat of frost.
- Marjoram needs well-drained, but damp, soil that isn't overly packed in partial sunlight.
- Mint likes rich, well-drained soil with partial shade.
- Nasturtium requires just average soil, but it needs to be well-drained and in full sunlight for best yield.
- Nettle thrives in a temperate climate and requires little fuss.
- Onion fares best north of the equator and can tolerate a variety of soil/sun conditions.
- Oregano needs average soil with good drainage and plentiful sun.
- Pansy likes sandy soil out of the reach of direct sunlight.
- Parsley needs good soil, good drainage, and partial sunlight.

- Pumpkin prefers hot weather but can grow well in a variety of soil and sunlight levels.
- Radish likes warm weather. Radish is a good window-box vegetable.
- Raspberry prefers light, well-drained soil with humus mixed in.
- Rose thrives in partial clay soils, especially if pruned in Spring.
- Rosemary needs well-aerated, dry soil with good drainage and partial sunlight.
- Sage requires good soil that's well-drained in full sunlight.
- Savory likes lightweight, well-drained soil in full sunlight.
- Strawberry prefers cool climates and damp soil but fares in a variety of regions nonetheless.
- Tarragon likes sandy, drained soil in partial sunlight.
- Thyme prefers lightweight, drained, and chalky soil in partial sunlight.
- Tomato enjoys evenly watered soil with potash. Tomato is a very durable plant.
- Violet prefers rich soil with humus in partial sun.
- Watermelon likes warm weather and well-fertilized soil that's watered regularly.
- Willow thrives in cool climates in damp soil.

Besides learning about what specific plants like, there are other bits of ancient wisdom that we can use in timing our gardening efforts. For example, try harvesting your plants at dawn to encourage hope or a fresh beginning. Harvest at noon to empower Fire herbs and flowers, at dusk for plants being used in magick for closure, and at midnight to invoke the power of the witching hour.

Additionally, when working with indoor plants, you can sow or harvest according to the symbolism of each season. Spring inspires abundance, creativity, and steady progress. Summer planting or harvesting produces greenery filled with energy for prosperity, power, well-being, socialization, and happiness. Moving your efforts into Fall attracts the vibrations of the harvest balanced against the need for pragmatic use of resources. Winter efforts energize plants with home and hearth energies, as well as those for protection and honoring one's traditions.

It doesn't matter if you live in a four-season environment. You can still use this idea by following the calendar or by paying close attention to nature's signals. For example, when the early-year rainy season comes, that could be your Spring, no matter what month is showing on the calendar!

Goddess Land Blessings and Protections

Gardening is not a rational act.
—*Margaret Atwood*

The ground on which we walk is truly sacred, especially when we approach it with a mindful, worshipful attitude. Goddess gardening encourages this gentle approach toward our window boxes and plots of land so that our plants and our lives might be fuller in every way. But beyond the way we think and behave while we're gardening or enjoying our greenery, what else can be done to bless and protect our efforts?

The ancients left us clues to this when they erected stones along the Earth's energy lines and around vortexes. The stones not only marked the sacred spot but augmented it. They not only adorned the land, but they brought people from near and far like a guiding beacon to the sources of power and transformation. Believe it or not, your garden can be like that.

How? There are some approaches that I suggest. None take a tremendous amount of time, but each is designed to bless, energize, and sanctify the work of your hands.

Sacred Stones

Do what the ancients did: Don't just toss aside those stones you dig up when working the land. Put them at the four corners of the garden to represent the watchtowers. Transplant them to the corners of your property to watch over and protect it. Use them as plant supports or decorative touches. Because these pieces of earth have been in your land for some time, they're already attuned to that region. This, in turn, helps them augment your magick (see also Crystal Goddess Techniques later in this chapter).

Asperging

Take a mixture of spring water and lemon juice (which has cleansing properties) and sprinkle it counterclockwise around the garden to banish unwanted energy. Then mix spring water with rose water and sprinkle it clockwise to attract positive energy. To this process you can add words of power (see "Words of Power," following) if you wish. Minimally, however, make sure you keep your mind fixed on your goal. Imagine pure, white light saturating the soil as you move.

If you feel like being really inventive, blend together the herbal insect repellent discussed earlier this chapter and use it for the banishing part of the asperging process. Note: This can be repeated each time you need to do a treatment.

Smudging

Native Americans use sage, cedar, and lavender bound together in a thick wand to purify and bless an area. This bundle is ignited and moved through the air either by walking the space or dispersing the smoke using a feather. This works very nicely for your garden too.

Smudge sticks are frequently available at New Age stores and herb shops. If you can't find one, you can burn some dry culinary spices instead. Ginger, onion peel, dried orange rind, and bay are good for cleansing and energizing. To safely burn a blend like this you'll need a fireproof container filled with soil or sand and some self-lighting charcoal or another fire source. Sprinkle on a couple of pinches at a time as you move around the planned garden space and let the smoke rise through the air with your prayers.

Words of Power

Magicians and goddess-worshipers alike recognize the power of language. Whether they are simply thought with a purpose or spoken out loud, words carry energy. Adding prayers or incantations to the previously mentioned processes, therefore, can increase their overall effect. Additionally, hearing your goals as you work helps you focus more fully on them, which also improves the results.

There are really no "carved in stone" prayers and incantations for garden blessings. I'll provide an example of both here, but please be aware that as long as your words come from your heart and are supported by the will, you're doing just fine.

Prayer. Stand in front of the garden space with your hands facing downward to channel energy to the land and say something such as:

GODDESS OF EARTH AND ALL GOODNESS, I COME
TO YOU.
HEAR MY PRAYER.
TODAY I HAVE STARTED A GARDEN WITH HANDS
AND HEART—
A GARDEN IN WHICH I WANT YOUR ENERGY
TO GROW.
BLESS THESE EFFORTS.
LET YOUR SOILS BE RICH,
YOUR PLANTS ABUNDANT,
YOUR SUNLIGHT WARM,
AND YOUR RAINS GENTLE.
LET THE LAND AND MY SPIRIT FLOURISH
WITH THE MAGICK CREATED HERE.
SO MOTE IT BE.

Note that if you're making a specifically themed garden you can insert the name of the presiding goddess and change the wording to better reflect that theme. More examples of this will be shared in Part II of this book.

Incantation. This incantation is for blessing the land, and begins at the Eastern point of the garden. I suggest doing this at dawn just as the sun's rays reach the land. Say:

KISSED BY THE RAYS OF A RISING SUN
BY MY WILL, THIS SPELL'S BEGUN.
WHEN GIVEN TO A WAITING EARTH
THE SEEDS OF MAGICK SHALL GIVE BIRTH.
WITH THE GODDESS TO GUIDE
HERE MY MAGICK ABIDES.

Repeat this incantation three times to stress the connection between body, mind, and spirit.

Laying on of Hands

Traditionally under the dominion of healers, the laying on of hands represents a transfer of sacred energy. Now you, as a goddess gardener, are also a healer of the Earth, even if it's only your little potted plant! It's very simple to give the Earth positive energy just by sitting down, putting your hands on the soil (palm downward), and focusing your intentions. Most people find it helpful to visualize a blue-white light pouring into their third eye chakra and down through their hands. You will notice the palms of your hands feeling itchy or hot, which indicates you're doing it right. If you want, combine this process with a prayer or incantation to improve the results.

Beating the Bounds

This idea comes to us from Rome, where once a year people would walk their land, decorate the borders, and offer prayers as they moved. The decorations, and the sometimes leaping dances, acted as an offering and incantation to the spirits of nature so that crops would grow tall.

Seed blessings

In many areas, including China and Rome, a priest or priestess would proceed to make offerings to the gods so that the land and seeds would be blessed. Traditionally this was followed by making nine furrows in the earth and sowing at least one symbolic seed for abundance.

If you find that none of these approaches feels right to you, don't fret. They're not necessary. Any altar (as a "high place") is created or reached more by attitude than altitude! So long as you work gently and reverently with your garden—with purpose, determination, and focus—you can achieve the same kinds of results as through any of these processes.

Moon Goddess Gardening Techniques

A garden is evidence of faith. It links us with all the misty figures of the past who also planted and were nourished by the fruits of their planting.
—*Gladys Taber*

The ancients believed that a Witch received power from the moon, which may be why many Wiccan calendars stress the lunar cycles so much even today. For the goddess gardener, however, the moon is also a symbol of the Lady herself. In literally hundreds of ancient settings, the moon was characterized as female, and Her names were many. They include Chia (Columbian), Hina (Polynesian), Luna (Roman), and Selene (Greek), to name just a few.

Beyond the potent symbolic value here, our ancestors felt that timing the planting, tending, or harvesting of one's plants could be more effective if we followed moonsigns and moon cycles. For example, when the moon was dark, it was time to plant underground vegetables. When the moon was waning, it was time to plant peas or other items that vine counterclockwise. According to most really talented gardeners that I know from the old school, this type of reverence toward nature's hints really works.

If you'd like to apply this concept in your own goddess gardens, here's a list that will help you:

Gardening by Moonsigns

♦ Moon in Aries: Plant garlic and onions, but nothing that requires really fertile soil.

- Moon in Taurus: Plant potatoes, root crops, leafy vegetables, and bulb-bearing items.
- Moon in Gemini: Weed and cultivate or harvest root crops.
- Moon in Cancer: Graft, sow, transplant, and force budding.
- Moon in Leo: Focus on deterring bugs using natural treatments and companion planting. Harvest items.
- Moon in Virgo: It's best not to do anything new in the garden at this time other than planting morning glory, honeysuckle, tulips, and endive.
- Moon in Libra: Plant above-ground flowers and vegetables.
- Moon in Scorpio: Plant vining greenery, berries, and grains.
- Moon in Sagittarius: Plant onions. Transplant and preserve your harvest.
- Moon in Capricorn: Plant root crops and tubers. Fertilize the soil.
- Moon in Aquarius: Cultivate, weed, and turn the soil.
- Moon in Pisces: Work with plants that require strong root growth, such as asparagus. Plant flowers.

Gardening by Moon Cycles

First Quarter. Plant annuals and vegetables that yield their fruit above ground (such as celery and lettuce). Green vegetables and herbs (such as cabbage and basil) seem to like this phase.

Second Quarter. Plant any "roundish" flora and vegetables (such as tomato and melon) and any flowering vines.

Third Quarter. Plant root crops and bulbs or anything that yields below ground (such as garlic). This Quarter is also good for fruit-bearing plants (such as strawberry and cherry)

Fourth Quarter. Let the land rest. Weed your soil, and then turn and fertilize it.

Note that these two systems (gardening by moonsign and gardening by moon phases) can work together nicely. For example, if the moon happens to be in Aquarius at the same time it's in the fourth quarter, this would double the effect of weeding and turning the soil. After the quarter passes, move forward with sowing knowing that the land is rejuvenated!

Crystal Goddess Gardening Techniques

More things grow in the garden than the gardener sows.
—*Spanish Proverb*

Stones, gems, minerals, and seashells have often appeared on altars to the Goddess as adornment and gifts. All things of beauty are under Her watchful eye, and crystals are certainly no exception. For example, old-time lore tells us that carrying a moss agate with you whenever you garden ensures an abundant yield. Wear it on your right arm for the best results.

Likewise, moonstone and lodestone are both said to improve any type of plant growth. Moonstone should go into the soil; lodestone strung around the border of the garden. This last idea is particularly interesting because it effectively creates a kind of miniature ley-line around your sacred gardening space.

Besides these ideas, there are several ways to use crystals to improve your goddess gardening methods, or simply make them more lovely. These include:

*Putting stones and crystals sacred to the goddess being honored in the soil or on the land as an offering and memorial to her.

*Matching the stones and crystals you choose for the soil with the energies of the plants to which they sit adjacent. For example, lavender seems to like the vibrations of amethyst. Both of these items are known for their gentle, calming effect. Following is a basic reference for stones and plants.

Elemental Crystal Companion Planting

This list matches the four Elemental energies of Earth, Air, Fire, and Water to common stones and plants that might go into an Elementally themed garden (or augment parts of a garden whose goddess has strong Elemental energies).

Earth. Stones include green agate, cat's eye, coal, jet, malachite, salt, green tourmaline, and turquoise. Plants include alfalfa, beet, corn, ferns, honeysuckle, mugwort, patchouli, peas, potatoes, primrose, tulip, and vetivert.

Air. Stones include aventurine, mixed-color jaspers, mica and pumice (or alternatively pale yellow or whitish stones). Plants include anise, beans, bergamot, caraway, clover, dandelion, endive, lavender, lily, marjoram, mint, mulberry, parsley, and sage.

Fire. Stones include any red- or orange-colored crystals and rocks, dark agates, amber, onyx, obsidian, pipestone, carnelian, bloodstone, quartz, lava, garnets, tiger's eye, and topaz. Plants include allspice, basil, bay, cactus, carnation, celery, chrysanthemum, dill, fig, garlic, holly, juniper, marigold, mustard, onion, pennyroyal, pepper, radish, rosemary, snapdragon, sunflower, woodruff, and yarrow.

Water. Stones include blue or green crystals, lace agate, amethyst, aquamarine, coral, geodes, jade, lapis, moonstone, pearl, sodalite, sugilite, blue tourmaline. Plants include aloe, apple, birch, blackberry, cabbage, catnip, chamomile, crocus, cucumber, daisy, elm, foxglove, gardenia, grapes, gourds, iris, lettuce, lilac, morning glory, raspberry, rose, strawberry, tansy, thyme, violet, and willow.

Putting this information together in one garden isn't difficult. Begin with a circular space. Sow Earth stones and plants in the North, Air stones and plants in the East, Fire stones and plants in the South, and Water stones and plants in the West. You now have an Elemental mandala and a sacred space, the center of which is perfectly suited to casting spells or meditating.

Planetary Rulers and Crystal Companion Planting

Each item on the Earth was categorized by our ancestors as having a ruling planet. If you'd like to do a planetary-themed garden, or portion of a garden, the following information can act as a guide.

Sun. Sun and stone plants are useful in magick that pertains to legalities, awareness, safety, wellness, the Fire Element, and vitality. Stones include amber, carnelian, sunstone, tiger-eye, and topaz. Plants include carnation, chamomile, chrysanthemum, juniper, marigold, peony, rosemary, and sunflower.

Moon. Moon stones and plants may be applied in magick for improving divinatory ability, creativity, relationships, fertility, and kindness. Stones include aquamarine, beryl, quartz (clear), moonstone, and selenite. Plants include cabbage, cucumber, gardenia, gourds, grapes, lettuce, lily, poppy, potato, and turnip.

Mercury. The stones and plants from your Mercury garden create energies for learning, applying knowledge, personal growth, communication, safe travel, and sensibility. Stones include agate, jasper, mica, and pumice. Plants include beans, celery, clover, dill, ferns, lavender, marjoram, mint, and savory.

Venus. The stones and plants ruled by Venus bear the magick of joy, passion, fortune, devotion, and love. They also are excellent for deepening the meditative state. Stones include calcite, cat's-eye, coral, jade, lapis, sodalite, tourmaline, and turquoise. Plants include alfalfa, blackberry, catnip, crocus, daffodil, daisy, geranium, iris, lilac, magnolia, pea, periwinkle, rose, tulip, and violet.

Mars. Mars encourages bravery, boldness, sexual enjoyment, safety, and protection. It also emphasizes the god aspect. Stones include bloodstone, garnet, lava, onyx, rhodocrosite, sardonyx, and red tourmaline. Plants include basil, cactus, carrot, coriander, garlic, holly, mustard, onion, peppers, radish, and thistle.

Jupiter. Although not as many items are found under this planet's dominion, Jupiter promotes a high spiritual vibration and understanding. Stones include amethyst and sugilite. Plants include borage, dandelion, fig, honeysuckle, linden, maple, and sage.

Saturn: Saturn is associated with magick for building strong foundations, protection, cleansing, and good fortune. Stones include coal, hematite, jet, obsidian, onyx, and salt. Plants include beet, elm, hemlock, ivy, morning glory, pansy, and yew.

Neptune and Pluto are not included in this listing because these planets were not known to our ancestors. Some modern metaphysicians are working on updating correspondences with this knowledge in mind, but fixed meanings aren't fully developed or agreed upon yet.

When you want to augment a plant's basic metaphysical correspondence with a crystal that matches that vibration, refer to the following information.

Magickal Correspondence Crystal Companion Planting

Intention	Plants	Companion Crystal(s)
Astral awareness	Poplar	Quartz point
Attractiveness	Catnip	Cat's-eye
Bravery	Borage	Agate (eye)
	Peas	Bloodstone
	Thyme	Turquoise
Cleansing	Chamomile	Aquamarine
	Horseradish	Calcite
	Lavender	Salt
	Rosemary	Clear Quartz
	Thyme	
	Garlic	
	Onion	
Divinatory ability	Dandelion	Hematite
	Meadowsweet	Jet
	Fig	Moonstone
	Hibiscus	Obsidian
Dreams	Marigold	Amethyst
	Onion	Azurite
	Rose	
Friendship	Passion flower	Turquoise
Gardening	Chamomile	Moss agate
Joy	Catnip	Amethyst
	Hyacinth	Chrysoprase
	Lavender	
	Lily of the valley	
	Marjoram	
	Morning glory	

Health (general)	Geranium	Agate
	Juniper	Aventurine
	Marjoram	Bloodstone
	Tansy	Coral
	Thyme	Turquoise
Love	Basil	Agate
	Catnip	Alexandrite
	Chamomile	Amber
	Daffodil	Amethyst
	Daisy	Beryl
	Dill	Jade
	Gardenia	Lapis
	Hyacinth	Malachite
	Lavender	Moonstone
	Myrtle	Rhodocrosite
	Peas	Topaz
	Periwinkle	Tourmaline
	Rose	Turquoise
	Rosemary	
	Strawberry	
	Thyme	
	Tulip	
	Violet	
Luck	Bluebell	Alexandrite
	Cabbage	Amber
	Daffodil	Apache tear
	Ferns	Aventurine
	Heather	Chrysoprase
	Holly	Jet
	Moss	Olivine

	Poppy	Sardonyx
	Rose	Tigereye
	Strawberry	Turquoise
	Violet	
Mental keenness	Celery	Aventurine
	Grape	Fluorite
	Lily of the valley	
	Mustard	
	Periwinkle	
	Rosemary	
	Savory	
Passion and performance	Beans	Carnelian
	Oak	Sunstone
Peace	Gardenia	Amethyst
	Lavender	Coral
	Morning glory	Malachite
	Pennyroyal	Sodalite
Protection/Safety	Aloe	Agate
	Birch	Amber
	Cactus	Apache tear
	Chrysanthemum	Carnelian
	Dill	Cat's-eye
	Garlic	Citrine
	Heather	Coral
	Ivy	Quartz
	Lettuce	Jade
	Marigold	Jasper
	Mint	Jet

	Mustard	Malachite
	Onion	Obsidian
	Peony	Tigereye
	Peppers	Tourmaline
	Primrose	
	Raspberry	
	Rhubarb	
	Tomato	
	Woodruff	
Psychic awareness	Celery	Amethyst
	Honeysuckle	Beryl
	Marigold	Citrine
	Rose	Lapis
	Thyme	Moldavite
Professional success	Clover	Bloodstone
	Lemon balm	Malachite
Sleep	Chamomile	Moonstone
	Lavender	Tourmaline
	Lettuce	
	Rosemary	
	Valerian	
Spirituality	Gardenia	Labradorite
	Lotus	Sugilite
Wisdom	Dandelion	Coral
	Sage	Jade
	Violet	Sugilite

Please note that this should be used as a guide only, not an edict. Each crystal and stone has a personality all its own (just as every plant does). If you feel that a particular stone should be matched with a plant that doesn't appear on this list, by all means trust your instincts. They will rarely steer you wrong.

The Language of Nature

All nature wears one universal grin.
—*Henry Fielding*

The Victorians loved plants, especially flowers, so much so that they created little tussie-mussies (bouquets) that had special meanings. The Victorian Language of Flowers provided a source for the meanings of the different bouquets. In this manner, the ever-proper Victorian society could convey worlds of meaning without a word!

For the goddess gardener, the Victorian Language of Flowers provides another set of meanings that we can apply to our thematic gardens. Here's a list of symbolic values for your reference:

Plant Meanings

Aloe	Protection or health
Angelica	Inspiration
Aster	Diversity
Azalia	Prudence, temperance
Balm	Social interaction
Basil	Fondness, good thoughts
Chamomile	Dedication, wisdom
Cabbage	Profit or prosperity

Carnation	Dignity, beauty
Cherry	Learning, education
Chive	Serviceability
Chrysanthemum	Cheerfulness
Currants	Pleasure
Daffodil	Hope
Daisy	Youthful innocence
Dandelion	Oracles
Dill	Happiness, overcoming
Elder	Compassion, kindness
Endive	Economy
Fennel	Strength, tenacity
Fern	Candor, sincerity
Fig	Improvements
Geranium	Joy, expectations
Hawthorn	Marriage, hope
Holly	Preparedness
Hollyhock	Fruitfulness
Honeysuckle	Devoted love
Hyacinth	Playfulness
Iris	Purity, bravery, messages
Ivy	Friendship
Jasmine	Gracefulness
Jonquil	Affection returned
Juniper	Safety or protection
Lilac	Love
Lily of the valley	Happiness restored
Magnolia	Greatness
Maple	Restraint
Marjoram	Contentment, happiness

Mint	Virtue
Morning glory	Affection
Myrtle	Fruitfulness
Oak	Courage
Pansy	Introspection
Parsley	Pleasant occasions
Periwinkle	Friendship, memories
Potato	Benevolence
Rose	Love
Rhubarb	Counsel
Rosemary	Remember me
Sage	Longevity, wisdom, virtue
Savory	Attention, curiosity
Sweet william	Honor
Tarragon	Devotion
Thistle	Independence
Thyme	Adventure, bravery
Tulip	Love or fame
Tulip tree	Renown
Turnip	Benevolence
Violet	Humility, fidelity, faithfulness
Water lily	Communication
Wisteria	Hospitality
Zinnia	Thinking of you

Please note that some of these interpretive values vary from book to book, and some are even the opposite of those noted in other texts. What I've provided here are the most consistent and positive symbolisms applied for similarly positive results.

Besides the Victorian Language of Flowers, our ancestors left other figurative systems to consider in our gardening and in the way we use our harvests. The first of these systems is called the Doctrine of Signatures, which was set out by the Swiss alchemist Paracelsus in the 16th century. The Doctrine states that the patterns and colors in nature indicate how a plant should be used. For example, a red plant should be used to help with blood problems, and one shaped like a liver would be used to cure liver problems.

Modern metaphysicians use this idea a little differently. In this case we take a heart-shaped stone or plant and use it in our "love garden" or incense, or potions, or whatever. Similarly, we might use a deep red flower petal to inspire passion, because that color is magickally associated with those feelings. Effectively this gives you options to consider when the specific plant you're hoping to grow or harvest for magick isn't available or well-suited to your climate.

This is where the Law of Similar, our second figurative language, comes in. The Law of Similars tells us that we can use anything of a corresponding shape, color, or texture in our spell as a substitute as long as meaning isn't lost. If there's no heather for beauty, then, just use another purplish flower.

Just as the Doctrine of Signatures ties into the Law of Similars, the Law of Similars ties into what is commonly called Magickal Sympathy. This concept says that one part of life's network can affect another part even over vast distances through image magick, such as poppets.

For example, if someone three states away tells you his child has jaundice, you might use a lemon to represent that child in a healing spell. The lemon mirrors the color of the problem (Law of Similars), it bears purifying symbolism, and the energy you put into the lemon by the spell helps speed healing (Magickal Sympathy). The sympathy between the lemon and child would be improved by a personal object being bound to it as well.

All this is a very long-winded way of saying listen and look. What is nature's classroom trying to teach you? How is the Spirit speaking through nature? How do these signals affect the way you plan, plant, tend, and harvest your garden? As you answer these questions, your goddess gardening efforts are bound to get better and better.

Fun Helps and Hints

Accept good advice gracefully—as long as it doesn't
interfere with what you intended to do in the first place.
        —*Gene Brown*

The goddess-oriented gardener gracefully takes ideas and advice from past and present "green thumbs" and then sensitively applies it to his or her own efforts. To us, history represents a great wealth of Earth-friendly, people-friendly, and practical approaches to what we wish to accomplish, so why not make the best use of it? Here is some pragmatic advice for your consideration:

- ◆ Put corn doll scarecrows on small stakes around the garden, adorned with some bells to keep birds away. Corn dolls represent fertility and prosperity and act as a natural representation of any corn goddess.
- ◆ Revitalize your fields by adding a blend of milk, honey, and olive oil to your soil and bless it. According to Roman custom, this will enrich the soil and bring life back to the land.
- ◆ Grow a hawthorn hedge around your garden to protect the energy you place therein.
- ◆ Grow and carry marjoram to keep ill-intended magick away from you and your home.

♦ Harvest your above-ground crops between 10 a.m. and 3 p.m., and root crops in the late afternoon, to preserve them.

♦ Harvest herbs you plan to use for magick on Summer Solstice so they're more potent, according to ancient custom.

♦ Save the ashes from your Yule log and mix them with the soil of your garden. These not only protect the home and attract good luck, but they are also said to improve plant growth.

♦ Grow chamomile in your garden and sprinkle a chamomile tea over the earth. This is said to create a positive magickal atmosphere suited to any theme.

As with anything in this book, you need not use all of this information. What is most important to your goddess garden is that there is meaning and joy in what you do.

Part 2: Goddess Gardens

Pleasure for one hour, a bottle of wine.
Pleasure for one year a marriage;
but pleasure for a lifetime, a garden.
—*Chinese Proverb*

If your mind is spinning with ideas and your hands are itching to get dirty, then you're in the right part of this book. I've assembled more than 40 different goddess-themed gardens for your playful consideration. Each garden includes the following information:

Histo-Cultural Information

This helps you place that goddess in her appropriate setting and often inspires ideas for personal adaptations on the garden's layout, decorations, and/or plants. Many goddesses had dominion over more than one area of life, and you may find yourself attracted to a different energy in the goddess than I was. Always listen to your inner voice!

Plants

If the goddess has any special plants that she holds sacred, they are noted here. Otherwise, the plants suggested are those whose metaphysical correspondences mirror that goddess's energy, and the overall theme of the garden.

Patterns

In magick, patterns are power (that's why so many religious traditions use ritual to raise energy). For some gardens, the pattern comes from the garden's function (take the clock garden, for example). For others, patterns come out of geomantic symbolism. One example would be using a square garden for the "Earth" garden because traditionally a square represents the four corners of creation, the four directions, and the four winds. Alternatively, a circle is certainly apt because we live on a globe.

Stones, Minerals, Crystals, and Shells

For the purpose of economy, I've limited these suggestions to those items that aren't overly expensive (meaning that I haven't included gemstones unless inexpensive cuts are available). As with the plants for the garden, the stones suggested will be those that honor the goddess or augment the garden's energy. They can be put into the soil, hung above a window sill, or placed on top of a firm dirt surface to sustain magickal energy.

Color

Every color has a specific vibration. That vibration harmonizes with a variety of magickal goals. The more intense the color is, the more potent it is. For example, adding a deep red rose to a love garden symbolically deepens the love being grown there. Consequently, when a goddess does not have sacred plants, or when you don't like the plants suggested for a garden, there is nothing wrong with using color to reflect your theme and goals.

Decorative Touches

Gardening stores have so many nifty products now, from statuary to reflection balls, that it gives the goddess gardener completely new ways to express his or her magick. The things I suggest here are limited to those I have actually seen for sale at stores or on the Internet so you're not driving yourself crazy looking for something that may or may not exist. Warning: Decorative touches can become addictive and hazardous to one's budget!

Direction

In both magick and feng shui, each direction has a special function that can support and increase the energy of your garden when used effectively. To this end, you can face the garden toward a specific direction, place a potted plant or window garden in a specific quarter of your home, or put a larger effort in a particular quarter of the yard. You can also use this information to determine where to put specific plants or decorative items to further accentuate your goals for the garden.

Adaptations

Specifically for those with limited space, this section provides ideas on how to honor each goddess and her powers in a window box, hanging planter, via potted plants, topiary, and so forth.

After-Harvest Applications

With all that good energy growing, it would be a shame not to use some of it! This section will give you recipes and instructions on using the plants you've grown for everything from incense and potions to magickally charged meals!

Why put the gardens together this way rather than providing step-by-step diagrams and details? Quite simply, this is more fun and gives you far more elbow room for personal insights. I have found that people tend to look to books as "experts" and directions as if they were carved in stone. Goddess-oriented people aren't quite as susceptible to that as some, but we still grow up in a world of black-and-white outlines that we're always told to stay within.

This book, by comparison, begs you to go outside the lines, at least in this one corner of your reality. It is my sincere hope that as you begin reading and trying different ideas, you'll enjoy not only the gardening process more, but get to know the Goddess in all her facets a little better through the exploration. Her ancient face is right before you in every tree and stone—dare to look. Dare to try. Dare to believe.

May your green thumb grow even greener!

Amaterasu:
Garden of the Sun

Climb the mountains and get their good tidings.
Nature's peace will flow into you as sunshine flows
into trees. The winds will blow their own freshness
into you, and the storms their energy, while cares
will drop away from you like the leaves of Autumn.
—*John Muir*

Histo-Cultural Information

Amaterasu comes to us from Japan, specifically the Shinto
Buddhist tradition. Her name means shining heaven. She rules
all other gods and goddesses and protects and unifies the people
of Japan. Not surprisingly, her emblem is a rising sun (as it
appears on Japanese flags).

At one point in her mythological cycle, Amaterasu hid
herself in a cave (this may have been a symbol of Winter or
perhaps an eclipse), feeling that the world had become too cruel
and barbaric. All the gods and goddesses begged her to return
with life-giving light, but Amaterasu was not about to be
swayed—at least not until Uzume (the goddess of merriment),
knowing how serious things had become across the Earth, went
to Amaterasu's cave and began to dance humorously, shouting
all manner of things to coax Amaterasu out. Uzume succeeded
with the help of a mirror that showed Amaterasu the beauty
she was keeping from the planet. Amaterasu emerged, Winter
was banished, and the light returned.

With this story in mind, we turn to Amaterasu to make a
garden of sunshine. In many traditions the sun represents
on-going blessings, something we can all use more of!

Amaterasu's magickal attributes include love, fertility, kindness, blessings, education, family or tribal unity, wisdom, peace, and charity.

Plants

As a sun goddess, Amaterasu's plants may be aligned with the sun's vibrant power. These include carnation, chamomile, chrysanthemum, juniper, marigold, rosemary, and sunflower. Bear in mind if you use sunflowers that they're very tall. These are best put toward the back of your garden where they won't block your view or create too much shade for the sun-loving plants surrounding them.

If you wish, you can include a few lunar plants too (Amaterasu was the sister of a moon god). Another alternative for an Amaterasu garden is to dedicate the land to growing edible items, because she taught humans how to cultivate food.

Patterns

A simple circle has been used to symbolize the sun for ages. If you feel a little more creative, make the image of a sun in splendor (that is, with arms reaching out clockwise to create positive energy). The border for this garden can be easily created with fist-sized rocks or another decorative edging.

Alternative patterns to consider for designing your garden include a kite or an arrow, both of which are Amaterasu's emblems. The kite can be fashioned pretty simply by making a diamond shaped border.

Stones, Minerals, Crystals, and Shells

Amber, carnelian, plain quartz, sunstone, tigereye. A neat idea is to pile some of these stones into a cairn-like structure to recount Amaterasu's story.

Colors

The sun's colors are also those associated with the Fire Element, namely yellow, yellow gold, red, and orange. Any plants, stones, or borders with these colors make suitable substitutes for those mentioned.

Decorative Touches

Consider a mirror or mirrored wind chimes (to create dancing music), woven fabric items such as small flags (because Amaterasu wove garments for the gods), or an iron garden spike topped with a glass sun or a votive-styled candle holder (the flame honors the goddess).

Direction

In magick, the sun's direction is that of the South, where her power is most noticeable. In feng shui much depends on what aspects of the goddess you want to stress. Look to the East for family unit; to the West for fertility; to the South and Southwest for love, passion, and energy; and to the Northeast to nurture learning.

Adaptations

Roundish planters set or hung in sunny windows welcome Amaterasu's warm embrace. Add some sun catchers nearby to literally "capture" and distribute her positive energy. Marigold is a good choice for plants, as it's very hearty and comes in both yellow and orange.

After-Harvest Applications

Items from Amaterasu's garden are best harvested in August, the month associated with her. Marigold is an edible flower that can be tossed into salads, soup, and wine. It yields a tangy flavor and brings a smile to most faces. Chrysanthemum and carnation can be added to this blend for a solar-flower medley suited to a Solstice observance. One third of a cup of each of these flowers dried and powdered, blended with a pinch of rosemary, makes a wonderful incense for honoring the Sun, the Fire Element, or for celebrating any solar festival. Similarly, you could steep a few of each flower's petals in chamomile tea to be used for an energizing potion or a suitable libation to Amaterasu.

Astarte: Celestial Garden

Ideals are like stars: you will not succeed in touching
them with your hands, but like the seafaring man on the
ocean desert of waters, you choose them as your guides,
and following them, you reach your destiny.
—*Carl Schurz*

Histo-Cultural Information

Astarte appears in the near East as the Queen of Heaven,
goddess of the moon and night, and goddess of the evening
star. She also embodies our passions. Astarte's myths tell of
her descending from heaven to find her lost love. Much to
human and animal distress, however, this absence caused a tem-
porary halt of all reproductive activity on Earth (likely alluding to another seasonal myth).

Astarte's name is seen in Syria, but she appears in Babylon
as Istar and in the Old Testament as Asthoreth. In these settings she presided over love and fertility. When she moved into
Egypt, she became a protectress who bore a spear or arrow. She is
said to safeguard sailors and oversee equity in legal matters.

Interestingly, many historians believe many of Astarte's
priests and priestesses were trained in the art of astrology, perhaps worshipping her indirectly as they studied the skies. Today we look to Astarte to reconnect us to the stars, our wishes and
dreams, and our heritage as inhabitants of a very large universe.

Astarte's magickal attributes include warrior energy, pro-
ductivity, fecundity, justice, passion or sexuality, and success.

Plants

If acacia or lotus will grow in your climate, these are her
favored plants. Alternatively, look to plants that appear as stars

(aster comes to mind) or that have associations with the moon (such as camellia, gardenia, cucumber, honesty, and willows).

Patterns

One pattern used to honor Astarte is that of a crescent moon, which isn't too difficult to make with small areas of land. I've also seen crescent-shaped containers for sale at garden shops. Two alternatives exist. The first would be to design a star-shaped garden (perhaps using a number of points that you consider "lucky") or designing a garden that's patterned after an astrological figure.

Stones, Minerals, Crystals, and Shells

Agate was favored in Syria as protective stone, so there's no reason not to include a few in your garden to safeguard its magick. Because Astarte is a lunar goddess, look to moonstone as an alternative. Additionally the moon rules the sea, so seashells (which make good fertilizer if they're ground up) and a starfish would both be appropriate.

Colors

Red and white are sacred to this Astarte (the alternative to white is silver, which could come through decorative touches, fencing, etc.).

Decorative Touches

Statues of horses, doves, or lions, all of which were sacred animals to her, are appropriate. She is also often shown with a mirror, so reflective items (such as a silvery reflection ball) would be suited to Astarte's garden.

Direction

Magickally, the moon resides in the West with the Element of Water. In feng shui many of Astarte's attributes reside in the South (along with the color red), but her color of white/ silver is in the West. This might lead to considering a corner garden in the Southwest that's split along the axis with red and white flowers.

Adaptations

Watch to see which window in your home gets moonlight the most often, or where you can see the most stars (placing a planter beneath a skylight might prove ideal if it doesn't impede traffic).

After-Harvest Applications

When you peel the cucumbers leave five thin lines of green skin on them (equal distances apart). When cut, the slices resemble a pentagram. Mix these with a vinaigrette dressing and fresh dill for a passion-inspiring snack.

Dry and burn the aromatics from your garden when you're learning to read astrological charts, or when you want more insights into your birth sign and its influence on your life. Or, carry acacia or lotus with you when entering a legal situation to invoke Astarte's assistance.

Bast: Garden of Joyful Dancing

Dance is the hidden language of the soul.
—*Martha Graham*

Histo-Cultural Information

Bast is a cat-faced goddess who comes to us from the Nile's Delta region. All of Egypt honored her as a solar deity who was filled with fertile energy. More than this, however, Bast was known as a joyful goddess whose followers took great pleasure in dancing, singing, music, and playfulness. The historian Herodotus recounted how many of her rituals were accompanied with a sort of street fair, complete with merchants, masquerades, and all manner of entertainers. Local lore stated that taking part in this celebration ensured the participants of good health for another year.

The importance of Bast and her cats is quite evident in Egyptian customs. It was a crime worthy of a death sentence in most of Egypt to kill a cat. Additionally, thousands of cats have been found mummified in tombs, taking their rightful place near loving owners as greatly honored creatures.

The Bast theme is ideal for anyone who would like an ongoing visual pick-me-up. The daily grind can often rob us of the pure, childlike joy in living and experiencing every moment fully. Bast restores that joy in her garden.

Bast's magickal attributes include happiness, kindness, sociability, playfulness, humor, sacred dance, inspiring music, protection, wellness, sex appeal, and fertility.

Plants

Catnip and/or valerian are necessary in Bast's garden because cats adore these two herbs so much, and they inspire such whimsy in these creatures. Other plants believed to attract joy include hyacinth, hawthorn, lavender, lily of the valley, marjoram, and morning glory.

By the way, asperging your garden with a little wine is a good idea for your land blessing or protective rite. Wine was the favored beverage during Bast's festivals and was often accompanied by light-hearted flute music and rhythmic clapping.

Patterns

A solar circle is one idea, but whatever your choice, try to make room inside the garden or around its perimeter for ritual dancing. Move clockwise when you want to draw positive, happy energies into your life, and counterclockwise to banish the blues. Many of Bast's worshippers often celebrated skyclad (naked) because they felt the body was worthy of rejoicing, so if you live on a large tract of land or in a rural area you may want to do the same.

Stones, Minerals, Crystals, and Shells

Stones under the dominion of Leo are an option (honoring Bast's Lion aspect). These include amber and carnelian. For joy, amethyst and chrysoprase are traditional.

Colors

Black (cat images only), green, gold, and yellow are all appropriate.

Decorative Touches

Images of lions or cats (especially those made in black stone), her sacred creature, are ideal for this garden. If you find an image of Bast, drape it in a rich, green cloth.

Direction

Magickally, East best represents Bast with hopefulness and renewal, and South symbolizes her more passionate/sexual aspect. Feng shui seems to agree, placing health, new beginnings, and positive energy in the East, along with the color green.

Adaptations

Bast is sometimes depicted carrying a woven basket, so look for something of this nature to house your indoor plants. If you add some feline decorations, that would be ideal! Alternatively, make four smaller potted plants to mark the four quarters of your sacred space and dance in the middle of them. Catnip is best-suited for the West/Water, and lavender or marjoram for the East/Air quarter. Choose the other two directional accoutrements according to the aspect of Bast you most want to venerate combined with the plant's Elemental correspondence.

After-Harvest Applications

Lavender has so many applications that it's one of my favorite plants. Dry it and add it to any incense where you want to lift heavy feelings out of a house or room. Make it into a tea and internalize self-appreciation. Steep it in warm oil with which which you scent soap, or add it to your baths and saturate your aura with all of Bast's wonderful energies.

By the way, scenting soap isn't difficult. Just take a cotton or linen cloth and lay it in a box that has an airtight cover (such as food storage containers, but use one that you won't want to use for food again as the aroma will stay). Dab the cloth with the lavender oil until the aroma is fairly strong, then lay the unwrapped soap on top. Close this up and leave it for several weeks. Soap is porous and will slowly absorb the scent. If you can do this from the first day of a full moon until the next full moon, all the better symbolically for magickal "fullness."

Brigit:
Threefold Goddess Garden

Brigid, excellent woman, sudden flame,
may the bright fiery sun take us to the lasting kingdom.
—*Ancient Irish song*

Histo-Cultural Information

Throughout the world's religious traditions we find goddesses who have more than one face. If we compare this to the Christian concept of the Father, Son, and Holy Spirit being one Being yet separate personalities or aspects of that Being, the mystical equivalent for the Goddess becomes the Maiden, Mother, and Crone. Wiccans frequently represent the three-fold goddess on our altars with a cauldron with three legs. The cauldron itself is creation's womb, and the legs provide support for nurturing that creation. Additionally, the triune Goddess represents the main stages in our lives and the personality or attributes of the goddess change depending on her form/stage.

In Ireland, and many other parts of Celtic Europe, Brigit provides us with an excellent example of just such a triune deity. As the Maiden she invented whistling to call to her friends (and it is said that Witches can still whistle up a wind). As the Mother she invented keening upon the death of her son. She also presided over smithcraft, likely as the Crone, because the elder goddess cares for the ancient mysteries among which metalcraft was counted as quite sacred.

According to old bardic song, Brigit the poetess had two "sisters": one who healed and one who watched over the smith's fires. This is an allusion to the trinity that Christianity kept when Christians made Brigit a saint. In Christian tradition, Brigit was prayed to for health and inspiration, two attributes also seen in the earlier goddess figure.

February 1, Brigit's Day, continues to be a sacred observance on many magickal and Christian calendars. This is a festival of light, representing purity (namely the Maiden). August 1 (Lammas) is another time when Brigit is celebrated in her fertile aspect (or the Mother goddess). No matter the date, however, this garden is a wonderful choice for people wishing to reconnect with the feminine, or yin, powers of the universe.

Brigit's magickal attributes include leadership, inspiration, health, fire, the Fire Element, protecting children, handcrafts, compassion, and sustenance.

Plants

Beans were sacred to many of the goddesses of ancient Europe, so they are an option. For my Brigit garden, I have looked to her attributes in choosing the plants. Specifically, I have a beech tree for creativity, ferns and juniper for health, dill and garlic to protect children, and alfalfa for providence.

Patterns

This goddess's name means shining arrow, so an arrow is a logical choice. Alternatively, choose a cross, which was often made from straw or corn husk to represent her, and then hung to protect a house and its occupants from evil. Indirectly this also brings us back to Brigit's solar/Fire aspect, as the cross represents the center of the sun and the turning of time on that axis.

By the way, Brigit's temples always had 19 priestesses because this number represented the Celtic great cycle. You may want to integrate this number into your garden somehow (sections, number of plants, etc.).

Stones, Minerals, Crystals, and Shells

Coal (as part of the ever-burning sacred fires of the heart or Circle) is a good choice. Alternatively, use any three-pointed crystal to honor the threefold goddess or three stones (one shiny and new white stone, one pink or red and slightly worn stone, and one brown and old stone).

Colors

Generally speaking, white or pale pastels represent the Maiden aspect, bright-vibrant colors such as red (for life and fertility) represent the Mother, and dark colors such as brown and black are those of the Crone.

Decorative Touches

A small tended hedge around your garden would be very appropriate as hedges often surrounded Brigit's sanctuaries. If you can find a brass-colored shoe, this is one of her sacred relics. Many wells throughout Europe are named after "Brid" (her Irish designation) so a small wishing well might make a lovely centerpiece, as would any statuary of oxen, a boar, or a ram (all sacred animals to this goddess).

Direction

Because we're dealing with three different aspects of one, directions become convoluted. One idea here would be a circular garden or planter that's divided into three equal sections, perhaps so they form a peace sign (Maiden at the top right, Mother at the bottom, and Crone at the top left) or three parts one of which faces east and the other west (east is the Maiden, west the Crone).

Adaptations

For complete flexibility, choose a planter of a suitable size to the space you have, then put three coins in the bottom of the soil so your prosperity can grow with Brigit's blessings.

After-Harvest Applications

The best days to harvest the Brigit garden are the 20th of any month, as that was when Brigit tended the sacred fires of her temples. Anything from Brigit's garden would be lovely to decorate a goddess altar, especially one for Drawing Down the Moon rituals. For those of you unfamiliar with this process, the idea is to take on the role of the goddess and allow her energy to fill you completely during important rituals.

Cerridwen: Potion Garden

Double, double, toil and trouble,
fire burn and cauldron bubble
—*Shakespeare*

Histo-Cultural Information

Although Shakespeare is known as the source of this quote, Cerridwen had the idea for making potions in a cauldron long before he was ever born! According to lore, Cerridwen lived on an island in Lake Tegid, where she was diligently brewing a very powerful potion for her son. This potion was filled with all the ingredients to make him wise, creative, and knowledgeable.

Unfortunately, a young mortal by the name of Gwion accidentally partook of a few drops of the elixir and received all of its benefits. Cerridwen was angered by this and followed Gwion unceasingly. During the chase, the two tried to fool each other with shapeshifting magick. At last, Cerridwen caught and consumed Gwion in the form of a grain of wheat from which a child would grow. This child became the greatest bard of Welsh legend, none other than Taliesin. Talk about the power of making good out of a bad situation!

This has always been a favorite story of mine because I love music and tall-tales. As a writer I often turn to Cerridwen when I'm experiencing a creative blockage. For artists and dreamers in all walks of life, Cerridwen offers hope and renewal—both of which blossom in her garden just waiting for us to pluck!

Cerridwen's magickal attributes include wisdom, inspiration, the moon, the muse, Nature, spellcraft, learning, herbal arts, potions, shapeshifting, and glamoury.

Plants

Cerridwen was also known as the White Lady, any white plants are suited to Cerridwen's garden. Second to this, look for plants that you personally use regularly in potions. In particular I would recommend white roses, lily, white lilac, and white heather as having potential.

In preparing your garden, make an offering of cakes and wine to Cerridwen (traditional to her rituals), breaking and pouring these into the land to enrich it with her power.

Patterns

Anything that integrates the number six (six segments, six points, etc.) is appropriate, because there were six ingredients in Cerridwen's potion. Alternatively, you might shape the garden like a crescent moon, because Cerridwen has strong lunar associations.

Stones, Minerals, Crystals, and Shells

To stress Cerridwen's knowledge and learning aspects, use aventurine and fluorite. For creativity, use egg-shaped stones or green quartz.

Colors

White is the color best suited to this garden.

Decorative Touches

The four animals Cerridwen became in her pursuit of Gwion were a greyhound, otter, hawk, and hen, so any statuary of these creatures would be nice for the garden. The hawk might go in the East for Air, the otter in the West for Water, the hen in the North for Earth, and the greyhound in the South for Fire because of its speed.

Also, don't overlook the possibility of putting a large cauldron somewhere in your garden. You can let it collect rainwater with which to asperge your sacred spaces!

Direction

In magick, East is the direction from which creative winds come to motivate and inspire us. In feng shui, Northeast is the direction of learning, Southeast the area for inventiveness, and West the direction for the color white.

Adaptations

White heather seems to fare pretty well indoors, and you can snip this in such a way so that has six distinct segments. Place this pot in a window that receives moonlight or an Eastern-facing window to increase Cerridwen's energy in the plant.

After-Harvest Applications

Make potions, of course! The type of potion depends much on your goal, but if possible use six ingredients to honor Cerridwen. Bear in mind that ingredients should be edible if you plan to consume the potion. The basic recipe for most tea-like potions is one teaspoon fresh herb to one cup of water steeped. If you're using six different ingredients, I suggest decreasing the overall amount of herb used to about one-half teaspoon each and increasing the water to two cups so that the final flavor isn't overwhelming. Note: You may also steep herbs and flowers in wine as an alternative base.

Concordia: Garden of Peace

There is no need to go to India or anywhere else to find peace. You will find that deep place of silence right in your room, your garden or even your bathtub.
—*Elisabeth Kubler-Ross*

Histo-Cultural Information

Concordia comes to us form Rome where she is often portrayed as matronly in stature. In one hand she bears a cornucopia, implying plenty, and in the other she has the olive branch of peace. Spots where civil arguments were settled often became sited for one of her temples. Quite literally this goddess embodied the concept of honorable resolution and harmony between peoples.

Considering the times of upheaval and unrest in which we live, I would personally like to turn the whole world into Concordia's playground. But for now, building small gardens will help to foster her gentle, healing energy in this world and in your home.

Concordia's magickal attributes include unity, harmony, peace, reconciliation, serenity, and accord.

Plants

Harmonious plants include gardenia, lavender, morning glory, myrtle, pennyroyal, and violet. Dispersed evenly among and around your choices of these I would include plenty of white flowers (any variety you like). This way, the color of peace is mixed agreeably with the plants of peace!

Patterns

As Sixties-ish as it might seem, laying out your garden in such a way as to create a peace sign seems quite suited to this goddess's energy. Create the lines of the peace sign using decorative pavers, which serve the secondary function of holding any weed block or mulch neatly in place!

Stones, Minerals, Crystals, and Shells

The Roman art that portrays Concordia sometimes shows her standing on coins. With this in mind, the "metals" for this garden might be aptly made from a mixture of pocket change. Alternatively, use crystals whose energies augment the quest for peace, such as amethyst, aventurine, coral, obsidian, and sodalite.

Colors

White and pale blue are good choices for this garden.

Decorative Touches

Because olive will not grow outside the Mediterranean region, I'd suggest looking for a pottery cornucopia to use at the center of your garden. Fill this with emblems that represent the parts of your life to which you wish to bring peace and understanding.

Direction

Magickally I'd suggest West, because Water has a tranquil, healing quality. For feng shui, the direction of Southwest stimulates contentment, and due West is the center for harmony.

Adaptations

Another tool often shown in this goddess' hands is a decorative bowl (those used for offerings). With this in mind, large bowls (especially white or silver ones) could become your planters. To fill the bowl, look to violets, which certainly take well to indoor gardening.

After-Harvest Applications

Whenever the tension in your home has built up to a point where something must be done, Concordia's garden is the place to harvest renewed peace. Go to the plants and whisper a word of thanks to them for their gifts. *Gently* take a good-sized handful of flower petals from a variety of plants (just tearing them off haphazardly doesn't reflect the cause of peace!). Walk clockwise around your residence slowly, releasing the petals to the wind with an incantation for renewed peace and harmony directed to the Goddess, such as:

> CONCORDIA BE WELCOME,
>
> CONCORDIA BRING PEACE,
>
> CONCORDIA INSPIRE HARMONY,
>
> *LET HOSTILITY CEASE!*

Dana: Fairy Garden

> There are fairies at the bottom of our garden.
> —*Rose Fyleman*

Histo-Cultural Information

In ancient Irish mythology Dana ruled over the Tuatha de Danaan, the magickally powerful entities known as fairies. Her name translates as "knowledge," but it is a special knowledge: the knowledge of things that go beyond surface reality. She is also said to be the mother of the gods, giving her a strong matriarchal overtone.

This motherly capacity combined with a similarity in names indicates that the stories of Dana might be connected with Danae. Danae was an earlier grain goddess who protected the matriarchal structure. For our purposes, however, we will focus on Dana as a fairy queen and mother.

Perhaps one of the most whimsical gardens one can create, fairy gardens are tremendous fun for the child in all of us. But be prepared to have tiny items disappearing, to have things moved, and for the sound of laughter or bells while you work. These are signs that your fairy guests are just waiting to inhabit the new home you're making for them.

Dana's magickal attributes include communing with fairies, understanding devic forces, and knowledge of the mysteries.

Plants

For this garden sow plants to which fairies are attracted. These include foxglove, lily of the valley, hawthorn, oak, ash, rose, primrose, mushrooms, and clover. When planting your garden use straw, which fairies are said to like, as a weed deterrent.

Patterns

You could just let your imagination run wild (fairies love playful humans), but a lot of fairy lore seems to point to a circle as being a favorite fairy pattern. Mushrooms growing in circles, trees growing in circles, and circular mounds were often believed to house fairies so the same pattern is perfectly appropriate for Dana's pleasure.

Stones, Minerals, Crystals, and Shells

Fairy crosses and fairy tears are two good options. Alternatively choose stones that enhance psychic awareness so you can know when company arrives! These include amethyst, beryl, holy stones, and lapis.

Colors

The brighter and more varied, the better. One note, however: Some stories indicate that the color red keeps fairies away (but these are usually malevolent sorts that you wouldn't want anyway!).

Decorative Touches

Hang tiny, sweet-sounding bells from hooks in your garden. Fairies *love* music. You can also treat some doll furniture with water sealant and leave your guests some chairs, tables, or other creature comforts.

Direction

In magick, each direction has its own type of fairy, so what you choose here depends of what you hope to attract. The Eastern region houses Sylphs (the winged fairies). Sylphs are perhaps the most whimsical of the fey, having a very light-hearted demeanor. The South houses Salamanders of Fire. Salamanders are full of passion. The West houses Undines (merpeople), who have strong emotions, and the North houses Gnomes, who are very helpful sorts if you're not a lazy human!

Adaptations

Small pots of clover are probably the best bet for successful indoor gardening. These could then be placed on a table surrounding a doll house designed with your fairy friends in mind. To encourage visits further, leave a little cream or sweet bread, two favorite fairy treats, in the doll house on May Day.

After-Harvest Applications

Shamanic traditions tell us that the Elemental world has much to teach us, and therefore encourages ongoing communion with each type of Elemental spirit. Using some of the items from your fairy garden to honor the devas is one good step in this process. You can leave some on your altar, make some into incense, or scatter some to the winds just prior to ritual or meditations with this intent. Additionally, if your garden is large enough, go there to meditate and commune with the fairy folk so you can get insights into their knowledge of flowers and plants.

Demeter: Gardener's Garden

The trouble with gardening is that it does not
remain an avocation, it becomes an obsession.
—*Phyllis McGinley*

Histo-Cultural Information

According to Greek legend, Demeter searched the world
for her beautiful daughter Persephone. She was so upset by the
girl's disappearance that she tore her blue-green cloak apart,
turning the pieces into cornflowers. The sadder Demeter
became, the more the Earth suffered: Grasses browned and
leaves and flowers died. It was not until Persephone was
restored to Demeter from Hades's hands that Spring returned
to the Earth.

Demeter's name means either Earth Mother or Cereal
Mother, alluding to her food sustaining nature. Offerings to

Demeter were never burned, but given as they came from Nature's storehouse, so anything you gather here might be best used fresh or raw.

Demeter's magickal attributes include agriculture and gardening, arts, protecting women, renewal, nurturing, devotion, legal matters, cultural growth and understanding, and abundance.

Plants

Consider planning your Demeter garden between February 1 and 3, and harvesting from it from September 23 until October 1, both festival times honoring this goddess.

Grapes are one of the fruits often offered to Demeter, so if you have space to grow some, by all means add them to your Demeter garden. Chamomile, as a "gardener's friend," is also apt. Some plants specifically associated with this goddess include cypress, poppies, and sunflowers. Beyond that, your Demeter garden should reflect your personality as a gardener and what you most enjoy seeing grow from the earth.

Use a little mead and raw grain to bless your soil (mead was a common libation to Demeter). Sow on Wednesdays or Fridays, especially on the 12th day of a waxing moon, for best results.

Patterns

Section the garden into three parts, as some historians see Demeter as a threefold goddess, and the number three appears in many of her stories.

Stones, Minerals, Crystals, and Shells

Cat's eye and silver are associated with Demeter. Moss agate is another good choice, especially for gardeners wishing to develop more of a green thumb.

Colors

Grain-colored yellow (the color of her hair) and green and green blue (the color of her robes) are appropriate colors to use in your Demeter garden.

Decorative Touches

A basket or bowl of pine cones is one choice, often being found in Demeter's temples, and horse figurines are also good as one of her sacred animals.

Direction

In the sacred circle, North is the direction associated with Earth, over which Demeter watches with a keen eye. In feng shui, the Northeast has a predominant Earth Element governing any of Demeter's more "conscious" attributes (such as law or cultural learning). The Southwest is also Earth, but applied to relationship matters.

Adaptations

Demeter rejoices in any work of your hands, especially gardening—no matter how large or small. I would suggest looking to yellow, blue, or green as a predominant theme for the window box or for plant pots, but really anything that you will enjoy and care for diligently will please this goddess.

After-Harvest Applications

At the end of the season, the best way to honor Demeter is to turn the remnants of the garden back into the land to enrich it over the Winter months. This also symbolically turns all the magickal energy you've sown there back into your soil, where it can germinate until you work the land again the following Spring.

Ennoia: Thinking Place

The ancestor of every action is a thought.
—*Ralph Waldo Emerson*

Histo-Cultural Information

In Gnostic tradition this goddess embodies thought, specifically thought with intention behind it. Gnostic mythos places her as the creator of angels. The great mage Simon Magus said he received teaching directly from her in the magickal arts and in communicating with angelic beings.

From a magickal perspective Ennoia is very important, for it is our intention, our will, that drives magick forward toward its goal. Additionally, I believe that we don't spend nearly enough time pondering and internalizing spiritual lessons. Ennoia's garden is the perfect spot to do just that: to stop for a moment and quietly collect our thoughts and rediscover the power of ideas.

Ennoia's magickal attributes include meditation, contemplation, willpower, idea-generation, and sound judgement.

Plants

Ennoia's garden is filled with plants that support the conscious mind so that we can think clearly. Some of these choices include celery, caraway, grape, lily of the valley, mustard, periwinkle, rosemary, spearmint, and summer savory. Alternatively you might sow plants that will help with acquiring magickal sensitivity, such as celery, honeysuckle, marigold, mint, rose, and thyme. In either case, make room in the center of your garden for a chair so that you can gaze upon your garden during quiet times.

Patterns

The first thing that comes to mind is the image of an open eye, because this is what lets us see, know, and understand.

Stones, Minerals, Crystals, and Shells

Stones for strengthening the mind include aventurine and fluorite. Meditative stones include geodes and sodalite. Finally, those for magickal awareness include amethyst, quartz, holey stones, and lapis.

Colors

Yellow is considered by some to be an optimum color for learning. By comparison, meditative and contemplative colors generally run in the dark blue and deep purple range. Blue encourages peace about one's thoughts, and purple augments spiritual musings.

Decorative Touches

Spirals, mandalas, and labyrinths are excellent designs to use for meditation because they lead the eye to a point, a central nucleus, that often deepens the meditative state. Note that you could produce this effect with border stones that move to a central object or grouping of plants or by finding an item that has such a pattern imprinted on it (a large stone, for example).

Direction

Wiccans consider the East to be the center of thought and learning. This blends nicely with feng shui, which places the seat of learning in the Northeast.

Adaptations

If there's a part of your home in which you prefer to meditate, that's the region to look at for potted plants. Of the plants listed previously, summer savory and mint are probably your best bets for successful indoor fostering.

After-Harvest Applications

Take a snippet from your garden on days when you know you'll need to focus firmly on the issues at hand. Stick it in your pocket, purse, or wallet where you can reach it easily when you feel your mind straying. Rub the leaf or bundle with your fingers to release a little oil. The smell will refresh your mind. (This is especially true for rosemary.)

Flora: Garden of Edible Flowers

The breath of flowers if far sweeter in the air (where it
comes and goes like the warbling of music) than in the hand.
—*Lord Bacon*

Histo-Cultural Information

This goddess's name literally embodies the flourishing
Earth and all that blossoms. Her festival days in Rome were
April 28–May 3, followed by one just for the queen of flowers—the rose—on May 23rd. These are excellent dates to prepare your garden and invoke Flora's blessings on the effort.

The timing of Flora's festivals comes near the beginning
of Spring, specifically as a way of banishing the cold and bar-
renness of Winter. They were filled with unbridled revelry and
all the shenanigans we associate with May Day even in modern times. Additionally, they were believed to ensure fertile lands

and people. For our purposes, however, we will honor Flora with a plethora of edible flowers that can, in turn, be used for kitchen magick!

Flora's magickal attributes include abundance, fertility, gardening (especially flowers), new beginnings, and opulence.

Plants

Although this garden should be filled with edible flowers (a list follows) another good plant to include is beans, which were scattered at Flora's festivals as a kind of fertility blessing. Vines and fruit trees were also sacred to her.

Commonly available edible flowers include: carnation, chrysanthemum, clover, cowslip, daisy, dandelion, geranium, gladiolus, heather, honeysuckle, hyacinth, jasmine, jonquil, lavender, lilac, lily, marigold, nasturtium, nettle, pansy, primrose, rhododendron, rose, sunflower, tansy, tulip, and violet.

Patterns

To stay with the theme, I'd suggest a multipetal layout (either rounded or peaked petals) around a central point so that the garden looks like an open flower.

Stones, Minerals, Crystals, and Shells

Jade, lodestone, and moss agate (general gardener's friends) are appropriate, as are bloodstone and coral (to increase number of flowers).

Colors

All colors in nature are sacred to Flora!

Decorative Touches

Someone said once that the groves were the gods's first temples, and in this case I agree that less might be better. The beauty of flowers needs very little in the way of adornment. Let Flora shine through her handiwork (Nature).

Direction

Magickally, North is the direction associated with Earth, but East is the direction of Spring, Flora's traditional season. This secondary direction corresponds with feng shui in its designation of the season.

Adaptations

A lot of these flowers fare well in indoor locations. If you have allergies, use silk flower arrangements instead. Bear in mind that symbolism is very powerful in magick and goddess traditions. The thought and intent behind your arrangement is just as important as of what it is made of. Additionally, by using silk flowers, you're not "killing" a living blossom from Flora's garden, which is a good way to honor her.

After-Harvest Applications

If you have early blooming flowers on May Day, go a-maying to bring an unexpected smile to someone's face, and decorate your maypole with an abundance of blossoms as Romans did.

To internalize the power of your flowers, you can make them into teas, jams, sandwiches, salads, and soups. You can even put petals into gelatin! Although this may sound a bit odd to us, up to 100 years ago cooking with flowers was very common. They're also high in vitamins, offering a viable supplement to vegetarians. (*The Kitchen Witch's Cookbook*, one of my books, has several recipes with edible flowers should you want to try some. Another good resource is Cathy Wilkinson's *Edible Flowers from Garden to Palate*).

One of my favorite recipes is for flower water. Quite simply, steep freshly picked edible flower petals in warm water, covering the petals completely. When the flowers turn pale, remove them and squeeze the excess water from them. Repeat this step with fresh petals until you get an aroma you like. Store the flower water in a dark container in the refrigerator and use it in cakes, cookies, and waffles for a pleasing flavor and aroma.

Fortuna:
Garden of Serendipity

One of the healthiest ways to gamble is
with a spade and a package of garden seeds.
—*Dan Bennett*

Histo-Cultural Information

Although most of us think of Fortuna as "lady luck," she
was much more to the people of Italy. Here Fortuna presided
over each individual's destiny. She brought fertility to couples,
she determined how long children would live, she blessed gardens with abundance, and she even drove the fate of entire communities. Better still for those of you with little luck in gardening, Fortuna guarantees us of bumper crops!

According to myths, Fortuna was Jupiter's nurse, the
patroness of matrons, and the ruler of the bath house. Rulers
often kept gold statues of her nearby to ensure the well-being
of their reigns. This would be a little difficult for most of us to
manage without a healthy amount of gold paint, but that doesn't
mean that we can't invite Fortuna into our garden and her luck
into our lives using plants that accent fortunate energy.

Fortuna's magickal attributes include fate, chance, luck,
destiny, futuretelling, oracles, kismet, and providence.

Plants

First think of the plants that you associate with luck (most
people think immediately of clover). In magickal traditions,
some fortunate plants include cabbage, fern, heather, rose,
strawberry, and violet.

Patterns

Wheels and spheres are very common in depictions of Fortuna, and they're fairly easy to lay out on the ground.

Stones, Minerals, Crystals, and Shells

Traditional luck stones include alexandrite, apache tear, aventurine, jet, sardonyx, tigereye, and turquoise.

Colors

Gold and bright yellow are good choices for this garden.

Decorative Touches

Any image of a winged woman can act as a Fortuna figure, as she often has wings in ancient art. Beyond this, Fortuna bears a cornucopia, which would make a good center point. Another alternative is an old-style boat, the prow or rudder of which Fortuna steers carefully through life's waters.

Direction

I personally associate luck with the East because that is also the direction of hope and new beginnings. In feng shui, children's luck is ruled in the West, personal renown is in the South, and prosperity resides in the Southeast.

Adaptations

One fun adaptation would be that of creating a bathtub planter. In certain parts of Rome, women who wanted more luck (especially with childbearing) would invade the men's public baths, because that's where Fortuna Virillis (that is, virility) presided.

After-Harvest Applications

Make fortune sachets out of any of the plants from Fortuna's garden, adding a coin that bears the year of your birth, and wrapping all in gold cloth. Carry this with you to attract luck no matter where you may be. Fashion these during a waxing moon so that luck grows. Consider adding other ingredients that accentuate the area of your life in which luck is desired to the bundle. For example, if you want luck with love, you could add a little cutout heart to the blend.

Gaia: Earth Garden

After one look at this planet any visitor from
outer space would say "I want to see the manager."
—*William S. Burroughs*

Histo-Cultural Information

Gaia was present at the beginning of all things. Known to
the Greeks as "deep breasted" (a sign of both fertility and providence), she even gave birth to time itself. But this accomplish-
ment was not enough for Gaia. She was lonely, so she made a
son, with whom other wonders were also born into being,
including the animals and mythological creatures.

Throughout the Greek empire, any area where the earth
opened was considered Gaia's mouth. Here, prophets came to
receive wisdom. Such places eventually inspired the renown
Greek oracles such as those at Delphi.

Today, we turn to Gaia to support the Earth's healing and
to connect with the Earth Element, which supplies us with

strong foundations, practicality, nourishment, and steady growth. We may also turn to her as a teacher of such arts as geomancy and the reading of Nature's omens and signs.

Gaia's magickal attributes include oath-making and oath-keeping, Earth magick, and divination.

Plants

Prepare your land with an offering of barley and honeycakes, as was traditional on this goddess's altar. All plants are sacred to Gaia (as a personification of the Earth itself) but in particular fruit-bearing greenery and grains were esteemed.

Patterns

A truly diligent gardener might go so far as to pattern the garden so it looks like the Earth from space, or minimally one or two of the continents. Alternatively, just use a circle.

Stones, Minerals, Crystals, and Shells

Stones associated with the Earth Element include green agate, coal, brown jasper, jet, and green tourmaline. Also, plain rocks that come from your soil are certainly suitable.

Colors

Green, brown, and black (the color of lush vegetation and rich soil) are appropriate for this garden.

Decorative Touches

A cornucopia (sometimes pictured with Gaia) or a globe each work as a centerpiece.

Direction

In magick the direction for the Earth Element is North. In feng shui much will depend on your focus. If you're working for Earth's renewal I'd suggest East. To learn more about the Earth Element look to the Northeast, and to make peace in your relationship with the planet look to the Southwest.

Adaptations

Friends of mine had an old globe that they sliced in half and planted with vines and other greens to symbolize a revitalized Earth. The effect was quite nice. To get the globe to sit properly place it in a circular stand.

After-Harvest Applications

Harvest the items from Gaia's garden in Fall, when the Earth itself signals the harvest. Use them to internalize the qualities from Earth that you need or in spells and rituals aimed at helping you connect with Earth Elementals (Gnomes). You may also use these in spells and rituals focused on Earth healing.

You can make an effective divination tool out of a small herb bundle or even a few flower petals from Gaia's garden. Tie your chosen plant parts together at the top tightly, and let the rest hang down freely. Leave enough string loose at the top so you can hold it in your hand while dousing. Steady the bundle, ask your questions, and watch for movements. Up-down movements are a positive response, left-right are negative, and circles indicate no definite answer is available right now.

Gauri:
Garden of Compassion

Make no judgements where you have no compassion.
—*Anne McCaffrey*

Histo-Cultural Information

In Hindu writings Gauri is known as the golden one, and her name is sometimes translated as "brilliant." This title reflected Gauri's incredible beauty, as well as her designation as the sky virgin. She lives in the heavens watching diligently over newlyweds and offering her blessings to those in need of a little compassion.

In looking to your Gauri garden, think "random acts of kindness." Specifically, what can you grow here to use in gift-giving or as donations to food pantries? Charity and good deeds warm this goddess's heart and often bring the same back to you threefold.

Gauri's magickal attributes include marital bliss, new beginnings, grace, kindness, sympathy, fertility, and abundance.

Plants

Prepare the land with an offering of any gold-colored liqueur and honey, both of which were traditional offerings for this goddess. Any type of balsam is sacred to her. Beyond that I would look to food crops (vegetables) or items you use regularly in crafts with present-making in mind.

Patterns

I visualize kindness and charity as an outward-moving spiral that never really ends, because we often cannot see everyone it touches. You can create this pattern using pavers or stones as borders that slowly disappear into the ground at the largest end so that the opening (from where Gauri's grace flows) visually looks like it continues into the earth!

Stones, Minerals, Crystals, and Shells

All yellow and gold-toned stones are perfect, as are seashells, to represent an ongoing eddy of generous energy.

Colors

Choose yellow, gold, and white (with small accents of blue to highlight the goddess's sky aspect) for this garden.

Decorative Touches

This is purely personal. If charity and kindness could be rolled into a statue or decorative item, what would it be to you? Some people use solar images, because the sun is associated with blessings.

Direction

I consider gentle kindness as having strong Water overtones, so magickally I'd suggest West. For feng shui the direction of service and charity is Northwest.

Adaptations

Garden balsam grows quite nicely indoors because it doesn't require a deep root bed. Choose the yellow variety to stay with the golden theme. Put this in a sunny window to encourage benevolence in the home.

After-Harvest Applications

If possible, harvest your compassion components in August, the month when Gauri's festivals were traditionally held. Bless them and bundle them up, leaving them anonymously for those in need.

When you feel a little beat up by life, carry a snippet from Gauri's garden close to your heart to help heal your emotional wounds.

Hecate: Garden of Magick

> O lovely Sisters! Is it true,
> That they are all inspired by you!
> And write by inward magic charm'd,
> And high enthusiasm warm'd.
> —*Joanna Baillie*

Histo-Cultural Information

An elderly woman stands in the dark at a deserted cross-road. She bears a torch, and dog companions heel at the ready. This mysterious crone is none other than Hecate, the patroness of witches and goddess of the dark moon.

Some scholars believe Hecate originated in Thracian culture, where she was the great goddess of the hunt and a mother image.

In Greece, Hecate resided in the dark moon, or in the Earth, where she rules the spirits of the dead and presides over regeneration. It was often customary for Greek women to implore her for protection when they left home. Additionally the image of Hecate when placed on a door or near a house was said to deter wandering, malevolent spirits.

For goddess gardeners Hecate's glen represents a way of tapping into our own special magick and learning to use it effectively. Alternatively, this garden is an excellent opportunity to learn about the magick of Earth's greenery and how to apply it for the greatest good.

Hecate's magickal attributes include eloquence (especially for ritual or spellcraft), magick, transformation, spirit communication, the mysteries, and decision-making.

Plants

Prepare the soil with an offering of honey, which wascommon on Hecate's altars. Aloe, dandelion, garlic, hazel, hemlock, henna, lavender, mugwort, poppy, and willow are all plants associated with this goddess and her rites. Additionally, plants used to increase personal power could be sown into Hecate's garden. These traditionally include carnation, club moss, and rowan.

Patterns

Anything with a three-part motif is appropriate because this goddess could look in three directions at once (this alludes to a threefold goddess figure and the ability to see past, present, and future consecutively). In particular, the image of a key with three parts to the handle or head would be appropriate, as this is one of Hecate's emblems.

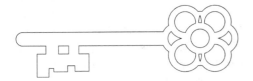

A simpler approach would be to lay the garden out in an equidistant cross with an image of Hecate in the center, or a cauldron, which is a generic designation for the threefold lady.

Stones, Minerals, Crystals, and Shells

Use moonstone and silver in this garden.

Colors

All darker colors, particularly black, midnight blue, and deep purple suit Hecate's garden.

Decorative Touches

Images of serpents, horses, or dogs, her three sacred animals, or a central cauldron filled with soil and some of Hecate's sacred plants, are appropriate.

Direction

This depends on your perspective. The center of the sacred circle is a type of crossroad where all magick comes together. But North is the point of "midnight" or the witching hour, which also would certainly honor Hecate's magick. For feng shui I've turned to the sector known for creative application of one's knowledge and skill: the Southeast, which bears the colors of dark blue and green.

Adaptations

My indoor Hecate garden consists of an aloe plant positioned in a small iron cauldron with an old skeleton key in the front (to unlock the mysteries of magick). When I have a particularly difficult spell or ritual in mind, I break off a bit of the aloe and rub the gel on my third eye and heart chakara to encourage working with insight and perfect love.

After-Harvest Applications

Oddly, even though Hecate is represented by the dark moon, her rituals often took place on the eve of the full moon, which might prove to be an ideal time for harvesting magickal plants so their filled "full" with energy.

Use Hecate's harvest any time you want to increase a spell's energy or your spiritual focus. Scatter her herbs and flowers around the ritual space to bless, energize, and protect it, or soak in a bath with them to fill your aura with wondrous magick. (Note: I've found this last application particularly useful for improving the results from glamoury visualizations and spells.)

Hestia: Kitchen Garden

Cooking is at once child's play and adult joy.
And cooking done with care is an act of love.
—*Craig Claiborne*

Histo-Cultural Information

The idea of a kitchen garden comes to us from the Victorian era. During this time people kept small, manageable gardens just outside the home (often near the kitchen). These little plots were filled with culinary spices, fruits, and vegetables so that fresh flavors and foods could be served when things were in season. It also saved the thrifty homemaker time and money, as she would not have to go to town and buy goods; she could pick them fresh and continue with other tasks instead.

Following in this tradition, we will turn to Hestia for blessings. In Greek tradition she was the goddess of the hearth fire, which is also the heart of a home and the symbol of family togetherness. One would never go puttering in another person's hearth without permission for fear of angering Hestia, who was considered hospitable and helpful to those she favored.

Speaking of hospitality, Hestia also ruled over public hearths—those used by bakers or those created for festivals. From this fire she could reach out and bring unity to whole communities.

Hestia's magickal attributes include home, family accord, unity, love, emotional warmth, frugality, and domestic success.

Plants

Before sowing your garden, make a small offering to the soil from your own dinner table. If you can burn the offering beforehand, all the better. It was traditional to place a little something in Hestia's fires to invoke her blessing on the home, and this extends that concept to your garden.

As for what you should plant, think edible! What spices do you use most often? What vegetables would you like to pick fresh and bring into the home for meals—or, for that matter, to eat raw? My kitchen garden traditionally contains beans, peas, cucumbers, celery, cherry tomatoes, beefsteak tomatoes, and green onions.

Patterns

An upward pointing triangle, a symbol for fire in a variety of settings (likely taking its shape from volcanoes) is suitable.

Stones, Minerals, Crystals, and Shells

For reconciliation in the home use selenite. Otherwise look to Fire stones such as bloodstone, carnelian, lava stone, obsidian, quartz, and red agate.

Colors

Red, orange, yellow, and some blue are all appropriate choices. Basically, think of any colors in a well-tended fire.

Decorative Touches

Hang lanterns or secure fire-safe torches in the middle of or around the borders of Hestia's garden. The fire within represents the goddess, and also acts to invoke her protection on your home and handiwork.

Direction

Magickally, South is the direction of Fire in all its forms. For feng shui, however, the direction for family unity is East, and the direction to nurture loving relationships is Southwest.

Adaptations

Within the home I would suggest using a self-enclosed candle near your kitchen range to represent Hestia. Dab this with some olive oil (something used in cooking) to bless it. Whenever possible, burn the first pinch of bread and other sustaining foods in the flame from this candle to invoke Hestia's presence and positive energy.

After-Harvest Applications

Many fruits and vegetables make wonderful natural colorings for candle wax. Beets are a great example. Take a little of the juice and add it to the candle wax before molding. Then burn this in the kitchen to honor Hestia.

Hina: Warrior Garden

I am a warrior in the time of women warriors;
the longing for justice is the sword I carry.
—*Sonia Johnson*

Histo-Cultural Information

There is a time to remain silent and a time to take a stand.
Our lives bring many situations to bear that make us face this
kind of decision between action and inaction, between still-
ness and combat, nearly every day. To help us act wisely in
such moments, we can turn to the goddess Hina.

Hina appears as one of the great goddesses of Polynesian
legends. Her attributes were many, including ruling over the
moon, guiding the dead, and being a fierce protectress of
women. She is generally considered a maiden and the first
woman to whom many royal families in Polynesia trace their
family lineage.

Hina's magickal attributes include vital force (creation),
safety, spirit communication, moon magick, renewal, beauty,
lineage, and heritage.

Plants

For this garden we'll seek out plants whose energies foster courage and strength. These include borage, mullein, sweetpea, thyme, carnation, mulberry, and pennyroyal. Alternatively, if you live in a warm-weather environment, go with traditional tropical.

Patterns

Any pattern with two distinct sides, as Hina had two faces (one in front and one in back), is suitable.

Stones, Minerals, Crystals, and Shells

As with plants, choose crystals whose energies support the qualities of a good warrior, such as sound defenses and bravery. These include agate, amethyst, beryl, bloodstone, carnelian, eye agate, garnet, lapis, lava, onyx, tigereye, and turqoise.

Colors

Red is the main hue for both Hina's warrior energy and her aspect as a Creatrix, because she formed the first man from red clay. To balance all this fire, add in some predominantly white flowers so that the warrior has wisdom and inner peace as an ally.

Decorative Touches

In one legend Hina reaches the moon by way of a canoe. She found she enjoyed the journey so much that she remained to live there. She used the moon as a suitable location from which to guide wandering souls who were lost in life, or after death. Alternatively, a wave-generating fountain would be a lovely touch, for it was to the welcome embrace of ocean waves that Hina returned to restore her beauty.

Direction

In magick, warrior energy resides in the South with Fire. This seems to correlate strongly with feng shui, which places energy and power in the South.

Adaptations

It might be nice to have a fountain with floating red flowers or candles to honor Hina's energy. I also found a nice fountain that had room for small growing plants. Because thyme doesn't need a great deal of root space, growing it is an ideal way to foster mettle and personal "backbone."

After-Harvest Applications

Carnation, mullein, thyme, and the other edible plants from your garden might do the most good if made into a tea, wine, or liqueur. The eating and drinking of anything made from plants allows you to "internalize" the spirit of that plant and all of its magickal attributes. Additionally, scatter a few fresh petals or leaves from your garden around your living space any time you feel like you might be under psychic attack to conjure Hina's protective powers.

Iris: Message Garden

I decided that it was not wisdom that enabled
[poets] to write their poetry, but a kind of instinct or
inspiration, such as you find in seers and prophets who
deliver all their sublime messages without knowing
in the least what they mean.
—*Socrates*

Histo-Cultural Information

Iris is one of my favorite goddesses. She's shown in art as glistening with winged beauty, using a rainbow to mark her passage through the sky. It is by this path that she diligently conveys messages from humankind to the divine halls.

Iris was assigned to serve Zeus, who often gave her missives for other immortals and people. She also acts as a handservant to Hera, showing tremendous devotion—even to the point of never sleeping or taking off her shoes!

This dedication to completing a task is the main attribute around which Iris's garden is fashioned. Here we will place all the blossoms whose aromas improve our communication skills and that motivate us to execute our messages to each other expediently, lovingly, and wisely.

Iris's magickal attributes include oaths, promises, prayer, communication, and generous service.

Plants

Prepare your garden with the traditional offering of dried figs and honey or crumbled wheat cakes. Into this, sow an abundance of yellow-colored flowers, as yellow is the color of messages. And, of course, don't forget at least a few irises, the flowers that bear her name!

Patterns

I can think of no more lovely pattern to use for this garden than that of the rainbow. Note that you don't have to curve the garden to achieve this result. Simply create straight lines of red, orange, yellow, green, blue, and purple plants.

Stones, Minerals, Crystals, and Shells

Aventurine, carnelian, mottled jasper, and sardonyx are four stones that have strong associations with communication and the Air Element. Alternatively, place seven stones, each one of which bears one color of the rainbow in it, in the ground. An alternative here might be to use a reflection ball, which often creates rainbows on the surface.

Colors

Use yellow gold (like the color of her wings) and the hues of a rainbow.

Decorative Touches

A water catcher is perfect. Iris would fetch water to use in sacred oaths. A caduceus is another option, because Iris is often depicted carrying one.

Direction

In magick, the Eastern Quarter, which also governs the winds, rules over our ability to speak and be understood. In feng shui we discover the Northwest being beneficial for Iris's helpful aspect, especially for serving others with a joyful heart.

Adaptations

My indoor Iris garden consisted of yellow pot marigolds in a golden container placed in a stained glass window that shined Iris's rainbows throughout the house. I also found a soft sculpture rainbow that I hung above the planter as part of the window valance.

After-Harvest Applications

If you use edible yellow flowers (carnation, dandelion, marigold, sunflower, etc.) you can pluck one petal just prior to an important discussion. Place this under your tongue for a few minutes or nibble on it to endow your speech with Iris's persuasive powers.

Alternatively, to get a message to someone you love, pick seven petals (one of each color of the rainbow). Whisper your message into the petals while visualizing this person, and then release them to the winds or moving water so Iris can convey the communique.

Finally, if you're tired of waiting for the phone to ring, keep a clipping from Iris's garden under the cradle. (Just remember to remove it after you get the call you wanted or the phone will be ringing *a lot.*)

Isis: Dream Garden

All our dreams can come true,
if we have the courage to pursue them.
—*Walt Disney*

Histo-Cultural Information

Born of the sky goddess Nut and the earth god Geb, Isis became one of the most well-rounded and written about goddesses in world history. Portrayed in Egyptian stories as a kindly goddess with a soft heart for humankind, she is credited with teaching people how to spin, weave, and develop other cultural occupations. She also taught women how to handle their relationships more effectively.

Isis's powers were so diversified that she received the designation: Lady of Ten Thousand Names. Under her wise eye, love could flourish, fate would improve, and the land was enriched. So how does she come by the reputation as a dream giver? In ancient times the Egyptians went to her temples to practice incubation. This was basically a predetermined amount of time during which people slept in the temples awaiting a dream (often one of a curative nature) from the goddess.

Consider planning your Isis garden on January 9 or February 5, preparing the soil on March 20, sowing on May 14, weeding and fertilizing on June 24, and harvesting on August 27; all of these are festival days for this goddess. Alternatively bless the work of your hands on the first or forth day of a waxing moon (especially if either falls on Wednesday or Friday).

Isis's magickal attributes include marriage (relationships), fertility, spellcraft, reincarnation, victory, health, arts, divination (by dreams), and wisdom.

Plants

Turn hair clippings into your soil to invoke Isis's presence before sowing your garden.(Her priestesses often loosened hair to increase a spell's power or used it in spellcraft). Other items associated specifically with Isis include amaranth, clover, cypress, geranium, ivy, lily, lotus, narcissus, snowdrop, and all water plants. Plants that inspire dreams include jasmine, marigold, onion, and rose.

Patterns

A star might be a nice touch, because one of Isis's names was Star of the Sea (and the star also represents the night and a place where we "hitch" our wishes).

Stones, Minerals, Crystals, and Shells

Amethyst, beryl, quartz, and turquoise often appeared on Isis's altars. Amethyst is additionally a good dreaming stone.

Colors

Gold and yellow are suitable, as is blue (the color of her eyes).

Decorative Touches

Any source of flowing water, which can symbolize the richness of the Nile, is appropriate. Alternatively, look for her honored animals, which include snake, eagle, cow, lion, owl, and ram. A third option is a knotted rope, as the art of magickal knot making was purportedly created by Isis. (Don't forget to bind your wishes inside, and release one knot when you need that energy most!)

Direction

For Isis's watery nature, West is best. For dreams, I'd say North, the direction of midnight. In feng shui Southwest emphasizes Isis's blessings on relationships and Southeast seems to encourage the creative energy for dreaming.

Adaptations

A boat-shaped planter would be ideal, because Isis protected sailors and is frequently depicted as steering a boat down the Nile.

After-Harvest Applications

Dry flowers and leaves and use them in a special dream pillow. You can make it any size you desire. For comfort, wrap the herbs in cotton bunting inside a pillow, and then place it near your head on those nights when you hope to receive important spiritual insights, prophetic dreams, or visions that you may need for the days ahead. To empower the pillow further, add an incantation such as:

ISIS, YOUR POWER WRAPPED WITHIN THIS SEAM
BRING TO ME A NIGHT OF DREAMS!

Iwa-su-hime-no-Kami: Rock and Sand Gardens

Talk of mysteries!
Think of our life in Nature-daily to be shown matter,
To come in contact with it- rocks, trees, wind on our cheeks.
The solid earth!
—*Henry David Thoreau*

Histo-Cultural Information

This goddess comes to us from Japan, where her name means rock nest princess. She is also called the goddess of sand, so who better to help us fashion our rock and sand gardens? As an interesting aside, Iwa-su-hime-no-Kami's sister was Konon-Hana-Sakuya-Hime, the cherry tree goddess who makes the trees blossom with such beauty.

From an Eastern viewpoint, the sand and rock garden provides the owner with a meditative space that can change and adapt with one's thoughts and vision. If you look at some of these scapes in Japan, they almost appear as flowing water made out of sand with the periodic rock jetty surging through. This is part of the wonder of rock and sand gardens—the ability to create beauty out of plainness.

Iwa-su-hime-no-Kami's magickal attributes include the Earth Element, specifically metal, stone, and mineral spirits.

Plants

In rock and sand gardens, plants are secondary. Use low border flowers or bushes and leave the central area open for your rocks and/or sand.

Patterns

Fluid and flexible patterns make the most sense here. Try not to get caught in any static mode, but find a way that your borders and interior can shift like the sands from which they're made. An alternative for folks who prefer some type of symmetry is a mandala pattern to which you're personally drawn. This should, however, create only the borders of the sand and rock garden; it shouldn't designate the middle specifically, because you'll want to change this part regularly.

Stones, Minerals, Crystals, and Shells

Keep shells tiny so they blend well with the sand. Stones can really be of any size, but vary the size and shapes so that the design can be altered with your whims and perhaps even with the theme of your meditations.

Colors

Neutral tones are best. Magick and energy is neither good nor evil, but wholly impartial. Its application is what determines the positive or negative "charge."

Decorative Touches

If you have the space to add a cherry tree somewhere near the border of your garden, it would make a lovely and aromatic addition. Note that weeping cherries do quite well in multiclimate environments and don't take up as much space as traditional cherry trees.

Direction

The direction of Earth in the sacred circle is North. This is also where the Earth spirits are said to reside. Feng shui agrees at least in part, placing the Earth in the Northeastern Quarter.

Adaptations

Several Eastern import shops now sell small sandboxes with rakes to which you can add a few tumbled crystals and points to create whatever effect you desire. If you'd like something saturated with more personal energy, start with an open-top wooden box (solid wood, not slatted) and fill it with play sand. Add specially chosen stones to this, and then let your fingers do the designing! (Warning: Do not leave either of these items in any room that cats frequent. They will use it as a litter pan!)

After-Harvest Applications

Because most of us don't harvest stones or sand, I'd recommend gathering a crystal or a pinch of sand during those times when you want to feel more grounded or when you're doing special rituals to honor the metal, stone, and mineral spirits. In this former case, carry the stone as close to your feet as possible (to keep one foot on the ground). For the latter, take the sand or mineral with you to the sacred space to welcome the devic energies.

Another good application for sand from Iwa-su-hime-no-Kami's garden is to help with sleep magick. Sprinkle a little on the floor around your bed to ensure a good night's rest.

Julunggul: Garden of Balance

Happiness is not a matter of intensity but
of balance and order and rhythm and harmony.
—*Thomas Merton*

Histo-Cultural Information

Another of my favorite goddesses, this lady is none other than the rainbow snake of Australia. Julunggul lived in any ocean or waterfall, in beautiful crystals and pearls, and in deep pools. What's most interesting about this goddess is her ability to appear as a man, a woman, or a wholly androgenous being at will.

Julunggul presided over many aspects of a person's spiritual life. In our garden, however, we will be looking to her to teach us the valuable lesson of balance in all things, especially within ourselves. Through this goddess we can discover our masculine and feminine selves, and the symmetry between the two. We can rediscover harmony between the spiritual and temporal worlds. At that sacred point of balance between sounds and silence, between breaths, between day and darkness, is magick!

Julunggul'a magickal attributes include cycles, initiation, balance, creation, culture, rites of passage, rain and water magick, shamanic training, and the dreamtime.

Plants

Whatever you choose for your garden, make sure to use equal numbers of traditionally male (basil, bean, cactus, carrot, celery, clover, dandelion, garlic, hops, lavender, marigold, mint, etc.) and female plants (amaranth, aster, lemon balm, blackberry, cabbage, gardenia, hyacinth, lily, myrtle, periwinkle, rose, etc.). Alternatively, use equal numbers of Elemental plants (Earth, Air, Fire, Water). (For a partial list of plants by their predominant Element, refer to pages 41-42.) This approach maintains the balance of overall energy in the garden so it can radiate into your life.

Patterns

Although it comes from another culture, a yin-yang pattern certainly embodies the spirit of this goddess. Another figure used to represent equality and balance is an equidistant cross. Finally, you could lay this garden out in the image of a snake out of rainbow-colored flowers.

Stones, Minerals, Crystals, and Shells

Shells from the ocean, water-worn stones, and any crystals are the best choices. Two-toned flourite might be ideal.

Colors

Balance ocre red, which represents life's blood, with white to maintain symmetry.

Decorative Touches

Two-faced statues, two-sided items, and two-toned items all come to mind. The key is that the visual effect of this garden needs to be as symmetrical as the goddess herself.

Direction

Magickally speaking, the center of the circle is where all magick takes place and where all the Elements dance together in equity to create that special energy. In feng shui, West is the direction of harmony.

Adaptations

It might be really fun (and somewhat challenging) to see if you can adapt a set of scales into a planter. This illustrates the goddess's balancing energies, while also symbolically helping that energy "grow" through the plants you've chosen.

After-Harvest Applications

On those days when life seems topsy-turvy and you need to regain a sense of stability, take two petals each from one male and one female plant. Place one of each in your shoes so that balance walks with you.

Juno: Marriage Garden

Keep your eyes wide open before
marriage, and half-shut afterwards.
—*Benjamin Franklin*

Histo-Cultural Information

In Roman mythology Juno was the faithful and wise wife to Jupiter. Throughout the empire Juno was honored as the protectress of marital bliss, especially for women. She also had several other aspects. These include Pronuba (who presents the bride to the groom), Lucina (a birth goddess who stands at the gates of life to assist the newborn), Juno Regina (the protectress of Rome), and Moneta (the goddess of memories or warnings, depending on whose translation you read).

Juno actually originated in Etruscan tradition. Her Greek counterpart is Hera. The month of June still bears her name and was the traditional month for happy marriages in ancient Rome. (It's interesting to note that June continues to be the most popular month for marriage even today.)

Today's goddess gardener can turn to Juno to strengthen his or her relationships with a "significant other." Marriages face a lot of pressures today, and we can certainly use Juno's wisdom and help to make the path smoother.

Juno's magickal attributes include lunar magick, protection (especially for women and children), marriage, kinship, and fertility.

Plants

Plan your garden on February 1 or 2, choose seeds on March 7, sow on June 1 or 2, weed and tend on July 7 or 8, and turn the soil on November 13. All of these dates commemorate festivals for Juno.

Plants associated with Juno include fig tree, iris, lily, lotus, and lettuce. Other plants associated with marriage include clover, lavender, myrtle, orange and lemon blossoms, rose, and rosemary.

Patterns

A pattern of three interlocking circles, representing you, your partner, and the unity between you that creates the sacred "we," is appropriate. It also dramatically shows that individuality is not lost in a union. Rather, two individuals create something greater than themselves!

Stones, Minerals, Crystals, and Shells

Coins are one option, because an ancient coin mint was part of Moneta's temple. In fact, the designation Moneta came to mean "coin" after a while. Sardonyx is another option, because of its association with marital happiness.

Colors

This is purely personal. What is the color of your love?

Decorative Touches

Eagle, goose, or peacock statuary would please Juno, as all three animals were sacred to her (particularly goose and peacock).

Direction

Magickally, South is the center of warm emotions and love. In feng shui East represents "family" and Southwest is the center for loving relationships.

Adaptations

If you've got the space, put a potted decorative fig tree near your heart so that the image of Juno is always warm, just as you wish the emotions in your marriage to remain warm and tender. Alternatively, find a planter onto which you can affix a picture of you and your partner. Plant tea roses in this container and keep it near your hearth, which is the heart of a home. (The kitchen stove is an appropriate substitute if you don't have a fireplace.)

After-Harvest Applications

Harvest Juno's blessings on the first day of any month, during a new moon, or during your cycle (if you're a woman) to invoke her presence and power. Include these items on the altar in vow-renewal rituals, forgiveness rituals, and spells and rituals for family harmony.

Kefa: Clock Garden

Steady as a clock, busy as a bee, and cheerful as a cricket.
—*Martha Washington*

Histo-Cultural Information

In Egypt, Kefa is the mother of all time and is represented by the constellation Ursa Major. How appropriate! She rotates on the North Star, with its tail pointing due East at the beginning of Spring, South come Summer, West by Fall, and North in Winter. This is the ever-turning wheel, the one that Kefa set in motion at the beginning.

We call on Kefa now to bless our handiwork as we try to re-create a visual image of time's movement in growing plants. The Victorians were quite adept at this art, which is where many of the ideas presented in this section come from. By setting up our garden in a special way, we can literally "mark time" and honor its passage instead of letting those wonderful moments slip away and be forgotten.

Kefa's magickal attributes include time, cycles, succession, and creation.

Plants

Arrange your flowers according to the hours they open and/or close. The morning follows this pattern:

◆ Goat's beard opens around 3 a.m.
◆ Dandelion, hawkweed, and wild succory open at 4 a.m.
◆ Day lily, poppy, and sowthistle open at 5 a.m.
◆ Cat's-ear opens at 6 a.m.
◆ Lettuce, marigold, and water lily open at 7 a.m.
◆ Pink opens at 8 a.m.
◆ Chickweed, field marigold, and mallow open at 9 a.m.

Afternoon and evening hours follow this pattern:

◆ Hawk's beard, succory, mallow, and poppy open at noon.
◆ Pinks open at 1 p.m.
◆ Sandwort opens at 2 p.m.
◆ Field marigold opens at 3 p.m.
◆ Cat's-ear and bindweed open at 4 p.m.
◆ Water lily opens at 5 p.m.
◆ Poppy and day lily open at 7 p.m.
◆ Goat's beard opens at 9 p.m.
◆ Chickweed and lettuce open at 10 p.m.
◆ Sowthistle opens at 11 p.m.

For those areas where there aren't plants, fill in with things like low-ferns and evergreens.

The medieval people did this a slightly different way. They simply had flowers that represented specific hours of the day. On this clock a budding rose was the first hour, followed by heliotrope, white rose, hyacinth, lemon, lotus, lupin, orange, olive, poplar, marigold, and pansy or violet.

Patterns

A clock face (round or square, but with distinct sections for the hours in the day) or anything with a theme of seven (Ursa Major is made up of seven stars) is suitable.

Stones, Minerals, Crystals, and Shells

I would use 12 stones, one for each astrological sign (which represents a full cycle too).

Colors

This is flexible to your tastes.

Decorative Touches

To my thinking nothing suits this garden better than a sundial. That way, even when your plants aren't perfect, the sun can still notch off the hours to commemorate Kefa.

Direction

In metaphysical traditions, magick works outside of time and within all time, so the entirety of the sacred circle and beyond is its direction. In feng shui the point of the mandala (the center of the space) is probably the best choice.

Adaptations

It is very hard to re-create a clock garden indoors. The best idea is to look for a flower planter that includes a sundial and then make sure to place it where the sun can reach the dial throughout the day.

After-Harvest Applications

Want to stay on schedule? Need to be more mindful of how you manage your time? Kefa is the goddess who can help. Gather a petal from her garden and place it under a noticeable clock or your watch. You may want to add an invocation, such as:

> KEFA, LADY OF TIME,
> MARK THE DAYS AND MARK THE HOURS.
> MARK THE MINUTES AND KEEP ME KEEN
> LET YOUR TIME BE EVER SEEN!

Kwan Yin: Family Garden

Call it a clan, call it a network, call it a tribe, call it a family.
Whatever you call it, whoever you are, you need one.
—*Jane Howard*

Histo-Cultural Information

Kwan Yin is to Eastern mysticism what Mary is to Christianity. She is a very compassionate goddess concerned with humankind's development and happiness. In fact, her name means she who hears the world weeping. Some stories say that Kwan Yin gave up living in the immortal realms so that she could stay on earth and help humans obtain enlightenment. In Kwan Yin's spirit, her servants were dedicated to acts of mercy and lived peaceful lives, never eating meat so that animals would be given similar kindness as humans.

The art of the far East is, not surprisingly, filled with beautiful depictions of this kindly woman. She wears beautiful garments and gold necklaces, holds jewels and willow branches, and is often accompanied by a male child and a dragon girl. Many people continue to use her name and her statue as a focus for meditations directed toward the goals of harmony, happiness, and kinship.

Kwan Yin's magickal attributes include fertility, healing, family, home, kindness, compassion, magickal learning, prayer, and enlightenment.

Plants

Willow trees are sacred to Kwan Yin. Beyond this, look to plants that inspire harmony, such as gardenia, lavender, loosestrife, meadowsweet, myrtle, morning glory, mint, and violet.

Patterns

A lotus pattern, on which she is often seated, is a good choice.

Stones, Minerals, Crystals, and Shells

Similar to the plants in Kwan Yin's garden, the crystals should encourage peace and wisdom in our relations. Some options include amethyst, aventurine, carnelian, coral, obsidian, rhodonite, sodalite, jade and sugilite.

Colors

White and gold are two colors sacred to Kwan Yin, likely alluding to peace. However, any hues that represent harmony and accord to you can also be used.

Decorative Touches

A statue of a lion (Kwan Yin is sometimes shown riding a lion) or a child (which she often carries in her arms) would be suitable. Oddly enough, many statues of Mary bear a striking resemblance to Kwan Yin but for facial features.

Direction

Kwan Yin's fertile, healing nature has strong lunar overtones, placing her magickally in the West with Water. In feng shui, the family garden should feature a family portrait (symbolic or literal) in the East or be situated in that direction to best support the energy you're creating.

Adaptations

Put together any type of window box or plant pot you desire and place it neatly under a rainbow sun catcher (one story tells of Kwan Yin visiting heaven by a rainbow).

After-Harvest Applications

Take blends of items from the garden, dry them, and powder them finely. Mix one tablespoon of the powder with one-quarter cup of cornstarch and sprinkle this on your carpets. Let it absorb all negativity, and then vacuum it neatly away!

Lakshmi: Money Garden

All money is a matter of belief.
—*Adam Smith*

Histo-Cultural Information

Lakshmi is a preeminent goddess from India who personifies abundance and wealth in all its forms. All things plush, beautiful, lavish, sumptuous, costly, and extravagant are under her dominion. Perhaps even more importantly to magick, Lakshmi is an active force for change. Vishnu's abilities remain passive unless Lakshmi motivates his powers.

Although on the surface it may seem that the quest for spirituality is very different than one focused on prosperity, in Lakshmi's garden the two can grow together. For one thing, though money may not buy happiness, it certainly makes many situations in life much easier to bear. Additionally, if you're not always worried about paying the bills you can focus more fully on other parts of your life that you want to develop, such as your relationship with the goddess.

Bear in mind that the Divine rarely gives out gifts without some honest effort on our part. But when your heart is in the right place, and your hands willing to work, the goddess can meet—and even exceed—our needs. This creates a partnership between you and the universe, where—with Lakshmi's guidance—you can achieve your goals in karmically wise ways.

Lakshmi's magickal attributes include luck, success, money, beauty, and abundance.

Plants

Ivy, lily, lotus, and willow are sacred to Lakshmi. Other plants associated with monetary gains include alfalfa, basil, chamomile, dill, clover, fern, grape, honesty, jasmine, kelp (which might be used as a soil nutrient), marjoram, mint, onion, pine, poppy, sesame, and vervain.

Patterns

A lotus pattern (a flower on which this goddess is often shown sitting) is a good choice. Alternatively, anything with a 10-sided motif. (Ten is the number of Vishnu's incarnations in which Lakshmi was his sister, wife, or mother.)

Stones, Minerals, Crystals, and Shells

Seashells are sacred to Lakshmi, as some stories tell of her being born of sea foam. Beyond this, wealth-attracting stones include aventurine, bloodstone, cat's-eye, coal, jade, and tourmaline.

Colors

Gold and yellow are well-suited to this garden.

Decorative Touches

Lakshmi's festivals are light-filled celebrations, so some type of lamp or candle stand would be a nice touch. Alternatively, look for statues or other items that depict cows, her sacred animal.

Direction

In magick, North is the direction of prosperity being associated with earthly goods. Feng shui places it at the Southeast along with abundance.

Adaptations

Find a large seashell and use it as a planter for clover, dill, mint, and other small root-system items. Add a yellow or gold candle to this planter and light it whenever you need Lakshmi's attention quickly to help with a pressing financial matter.

After-Harvest Applications

September is the best time to harvest Lakshmi's garden, especially if you can have a celebratory dance, too. This was the traditional time when her festival was held.

After the harvest, carry leaves or petals as prosperity charms or steep edible herbs in hot water to internalize abundance. I also like to tuck fresh or dried items into my purse, wallet, and checkbook to keep money where it belongs. While doing so, I add an incantation such as this one:

> LAKSHIMI WHERE THIS FLOWER LAYS
> LET MY MONEY SAFELY STAY!

Latiaran: Fire Garden

By labor fire is got out of stone.
—*Dutch Proverb*

Histo-Cultural Information

The power and symbolism of the Elements comes to bear in both magickal and goddess traditions. In this garden we'll honor and commune with the Element of Fire, known for its warmth, emotion, passion, energy, light, strength, vitality, and purifying ability. Beware, however, as Fire is a two-edged sword that can also burn when left untended or misused. This dualistic nature is common among the Elements, which means we must use them wisely and respectfully.

We turn to Latiaran to help us in this task. Although early versions of this Irish goddess may have been seasonal in nature, her two sisters—whose names translate as "yellow-haired girl" and "flame"—indicate something quite different, or minimally another aspect connected to the hearth and fire.

Stories tell us that Latiaran presided over the harvest season, before the sun's power dwindled. It was she who brought the seed of fire each morning to the sacred forge, never being harmed by its flame. The custom of bringing fire from a matron's heart to light other fires, especially ritual ones, is still reflected in a variety of European folk dances and celebrations.

Latiaran's magickal attributes include abundance, the harvest, smithery, the Fire Element, and safety (from fire).

Plants

Plants aligned with the Fire Element include amaranth, angelica, basil, cactus, carnation, carrot, celery, chrysanthemum, dill, fennel, garlic, hawthorn, holly, marigold, mustard, oak, onion, pepper, rosemary, sesame, sunflower, thistle, and witch hazel.

Alternatively, sow your garden with plants whose colors reflect those seen in a fire.

Patterns

This garden looks quite striking if you can pattern it to look like a tongue of flame with red and orange border flowers. An upward pointing triangle is another traditional emblem for fire.

Stones, Minerals, Crystals, and Shells

As with plants, these can be stones that bear a bright red, orange or yellow color, or they can be those aligned with Fire, including agate, amber, obsidian, onyx, rhodocrosite, bloodstone, carnelian, citrine, hematite, lava, sunstone, and watermelon tourmaline.

Colors

Red, orange, yellow, and pale blue are all good choices.

Decorative Touches

Find a way to bring fire into your garden either through lanterns, incense burners, braziers, or perhaps even a cauldron into which burning items can go safely. When the fire is lit, Latiaran is present. (This is an ideal time to ask for blessings, empower your plants, and so on.)

Direction

Magickally, South is the direction of Fire. This idea is mirrored in feng shui, where South's color is red, its Element is Fire, and it's filled with energy.

Adaptations

I often use small planters as alternative holders for stick or cone incense. The soil catches the ashes neatly. While the incense burns, Latiaran and her fires can purify my living space, re-energize me, and improve the overall emotional warmth in the house. Alternatively, you can use the soil to hold a candle that you can light to welcome the goddess when you need her. Use a red, orange, or yellow candle for best results.

After-Harvest Applications

The harvest from Latiaran's garden is ideal for consecrating ritual fires or for using as the base components in incense, libations, and cakes/ale for fire festivals. As one might expect, many fire festivals take place during the Spring and Summer when the sun is at its height. Examples include Beltane and Summer Solstice.

To better invoke the energy from Latiaran's harvest, dab some oil made from any of the plants on a candle and leap over the flame. This represents the power of overcoming and a potent transformation from one type of life to another.

Mari: Moon Garden

The moon is the first milestone on the road to the stars.
—*Arthur C. Clarke*

Histo-Cultural Information

If you look at the oral and written history about magick, it's obvious that the lunar sphere plays a key role in our methods. From timing magick by the moon's phases and signs to Drawing Down the Moon Rituals that bring goddess and human into a unique oneness, there is no metaphysical tradition that doesn't include the moon in some way.

Mari is but one moon goddess who comes to us from Basque tradition. Each night she emerges from the Earth's womb and crosses the dark sky along with her husband. She rides a horse-driven cart or ball of fire, carrying a burning sickle. What's even more interesting is that Mari was a patroness of Witches, giving even more credence to the old beliefs that a Witch's magickal power comes from the moon.

In making and tending your garden, bear in mind that Mari expects much from her followers. She desires honesty, humility, and responsibility, all fantastic qualities to sow in your land, in magick, and in life.

Mari's magickal attributes include divination, Witchcraft, magick, and lunar energy.

Plants

Friday is a good day to consider planting your garden, as in Basque tradition this is the moon's day. Alternatively, plant on Monday, which is named after the moon. Fertilize your soil with wool snippets, as wool was a favored fabric of the goddess.

Lunar plants include aloe, cabbage, cucumber, gardenia, gourd, grape, honesty, jasmine, lettuce, lily, moonwort, poppy, potato, and turnip.

Patterns

Aside from a crescent moon or circle, Mari is sometimes represented by a tree or a rainbow, both of which make serviceable patterns for your garden (or decorative touches for it). The circle pattern, particularly, is said to act as a protective talisman for one's home and grounds.

Alternatively, anything with a seven-point motif is an option, because seven was her sacred number.

Stones, Minerals, Crystals, and Shells

Moonstone, of course, is ideal. Also, red-toned shells (the moon is associated with the Water Element), aquamarine, beryl, and selenite are appropriate.

Colors

Red is your best choice.

Decorative Touches

The ladybird was often thought to be Mari's messenger, so a figurine of that—or any other bird figurine—would be suitable. Other sacred animal figurines include that of a goat, ram, horse, cow, crow, and raven.

Direction

The moon's direction is due West with Water in magick. In feng shui Mari might be associated with the South, whose color is red, or the West where chi energy resides.

Adaptations

Find a planter that has red and silver highlights in it to honor both Mari and the sheen of moonlight. Sow your chosen plants in it, and keep it in a window that receives the moon's rays.

After-Harvest Applications

Reap Mari's garden when the moon is full for the fulfillment of all of Mari's best attributes. Use these on the altar during lunar rituals or as part of beverages and foods aimed at strengthening your lunar characteristics.

Alternatively, place some of the snippings from the garden into a tea ball or gauze bag and put them in a hot tub. Soak in the tub to absorb Mari's attributes into your aura, especially as part of preritual preparation.

The Muses: Garden of Art, Laughter, and Mirth

A good laugh and a long sleep
are the best cures in the doctor's book.
—*Irish Proverb*

Histo-Cultural Information

In Greek mythology the Muses were the daughters of Zeus. Early stories talk about only three goddesses of practicing, remembering, and singing. The later tales (which were much more popular tales) number the Muses at nine.

First comes Clio, the muse of history, who is depicted with a trumpet, scroll, and/or open book where all important events get recorded. Her name means fame giver. Second is Euterpe is the goddess of the flute and, by extension, sweet-sounding music that inspires joy in all who here it. Thalia is the third muse, a goddess of humor and comedy shown wearing an amusing mask. Her name means festive. Fourth, Melpomene is the goddess of great tragic stories who wears the tragedy mask (frowning) and whose sacred plant is the vine. Fifth, Terpsichore governs lyrical poetry and dance with a magickal lyre. Erato, the sixth muse, guides erotic poets to pen and pad. Just by reading her words, one's desires are said to be awakened! The seventh muse, Polyhymnia, is a goddess of mime and hymns who is portrayed asking for silence by a finger to her lips. Urania, the eighth muse, oversees astronomical arts using a globe of the heavens and a compass. The ninth muse, Calliope, is another poetess who inspires epics. She also helps in the area of eloquent communications. Her tools are tablets and a stylus. Though each of these sisters had an important role to play in the Greek tradition, Calliope seemed more favored.

Overall we look to these nine sisters to bring more beauty and pleasure into our somewhat concrete world. For artists of any sort, a muse garden can help inspire and motivate real genius and unique works. And even those who may not consider themselves creative can be touched by the encouraging nature of muse energy that reaches out and shows us how to enjoy the arts, and even develop our own artistic voice where none existed before.

The goddess's magickal attributes include creativity, inspiration, motivation, the arts, and artistic expression.

Plants

Any bee-attracting flower is one option, as honey was believed to bear creative energy especially when used in brewing. Other plants noted for inspiring properties include ash tree and lotus flower.

Patterns

This is definitely the garden where your imagination should be allowed to run wild. Don't think in static terms, but look at your garden as an ongoing creative outlet that you can tweak and hone as the Muses strike!

Stones, Minerals, Crystals, and Shells

Stones and crystals associated with the Water Element (such as amethyst, coral, and moonstone) often improve creative flow. Those associated with Air (such as aventurine, mica, and pumice) often bear all the right energy to help generate fresh ideas.

Colors

Magickally speaking, yellow is the color of creativity and inspiration.

Decorative Touches

A central decorative willow would be a wonderful touch, as willow wands were sometimes used to invoke the Muses. Beyond that look to all the tools of the Muses as possibilities to accent your garden. I also strongly suggest making a spot for yourself to sit and enjoy this special place, leaving enough room to work on whatever art inspires you the most. This honors the Muses and gives them a chance to bless your work.

Direction

West is the direction to release a wave of pure creativity; East is the direction in which the winds of change can gently manifest new concepts in your art. In feng shui the direction for inventiveness is Southeast. However, if you would like to be recognized for your art, a better choice is the South.

Adaptations

Take a large planter filled with vines and add some small goddess images to it (nine if possible). Put these around the edges of the planter with one representing Calliope in the middle to direct beneficial cosmic melodies into your living space.

🀆🀆🀆🀆🀆🀆🀆🀆🀆🀆🀆

🀆🀆🀆🀆🀆🀆🀆🀆🀆🀆🀆

After-Harvest Applications

Bring a fresh bundle of plants gathered from your garden into the house any time you need a fresh outlook on something. Note that this doesn't have to just be an art. Inventiveness extends to creative problem-solving, too!

Leave some of these near the area where you most need the Muses's inspiration (like at an artist's table). Dab oils made from the flowers on a candle and light it each time you need to light up some ideas. This seems to help a lot with creative blockage as a combination spell and aromatherapy method.

The Norns: Garden of Destiny

Destiny is not a matter of chance; it is a matter of choice.
It is not a thing to he waited for; it is a thing to be achieved.
—*William Jennings Bryan*

Histo-Cultural Information

In a land far across time's veil, beneath the World Tree, one may find three Scandinavian goddesses. They are sisters whose power is not to be questioned even by other gods. Their names were Urd, Verdandi, and Skuld. Every morning the Norn sisters watered the World Tree from Urd's well. Never was too much or too little given, for this tree's roots nourish the world.

Though the task of tending the World Tree would seem important enough, these goddesses's duties did not end there. In their charge was each person's destiny: when one was born, how long they lived, how fortunate and talented they were, and when life's thread was finally cut. By extension, they also presided over the past (Urd), present (Verdandi), and future (Skuld) of all things.

For those of us looking to improve our fate, then, pleasing the Norns might be a lovely way of doing it! The best time to plan your garden is on New Year's (be that the mundane New Year of January 1 or the magickal one of Halloween). This was their traditional festival date, which is why to this day so many customs exist about changing the fate for the coming year.

The Norns's magickal attributes include fate, kismit, birth, death, fortune, serendipity, skill, and achievement.

Plants

Consider those plants that represent the area of your life where you most wish the Norn sisters's assistance. For example, if you're longing for a lifemate, plant the flowers of love so that fate may bring the right person your way.

Patterns

Because this goddess has three aspects, any tri-foil motif would be apt. Make sure that this garden has a good symmetry so none of the sisters feels overshadowed. One such symbol integrates three triangles joined in the center at their points, which is often used to represent fate.

A third image associated with the sisters is a downward pointing triangle with three circles (one at each side).

Stones, Minerals, Crystals, and Shells

Match your stones to the theme of your plants for best results. Alternatively look to things that speak of the aeons, such as geodes and holy stones.

Colors

This is totally flexible. I recommend a blend so that the garden is as diversified as life itself!

Decorative Touches

Any woven items to represent fate's thread and how it touches on so many things we do not see are suitable. Alternatively, have a wishing well or a tree as the central point in your garden, representing Urd's well and the World Tree where the Norns live.

Direction

Magickally speaking I'd place "fate" at the center of the circle or even beyond its normal boundaries. In feng shui a child's destiny resides in the West, renown in the South, and prosperity in the Southeast.

Adaptations

Find a three-legged container and sow it with your preferred plant. Add a small web affixed to a long skewer stick to this (to look like a spider web in the middle of the greenery). The web is a good symbol for fate and its movements.

After-Harvest Applications

I am one not to tempt fate by asking for too much, except when extreme situations arise. Beyond that it might be best to let your garden grow and turn back into the soil with time's ever-moving wheel. When real problems manifest, take a few small pieces from the garden and hold them while concentrating on your need. Thank the Norns and your garden spirits for any help they can provide, and put those clippings in a safe place. Watch expectantly while making as many concrete efforts toward your goal as possible. Your effort opens the door through which the Norn's energy can work. When the problem resolves itself, return the clippings to the earth with a thankful heart.

Oto: Water Garden

A great ship asks for deep waters.
—*Romanian Proverb*

Histo-Cultural Information

This Japanese goddess's story closely matches that of Niamh of Ireland. Being a sea goddess, she took a young handsome fisherman to her palace deep below the waves. When he began to wish for life on the land again, she returned him to the earth bearing a box that he could not open.

Unfortunately for the lad, time in the magickal realm of the sea is much different than on land. Hundreds of years passed and all that he knew and loved was long gone. He sat down on the beach in despair and rummaged through his goods. Without thinking, he opened the forbidden box. Here Oto had stored his years with her, so the young man quickly aged and died, returning his body to Oto's seas.

This type of story is classical and gently reminds us that the magickal realm is not to be toyed with unless one is wise, responsible, and cautious. More important to our theme gardening, however, is Oto's connection to water. Because of water's cycle, some of the drops that fell on the land in the time of the dinosaurs and the time of Moses still falls on the land today. This cycle of renewal, of immortality, is part of water's power. We invoke an understanding of our own cycles and the Element of Water in sowing Oto's garden.

Oto's magickal attributes include the Water Element, time, immortality, cycles, the seas, and beauty.

Plants

Choose any plant(s) aligned with the Water Element of water, such as aloe, aster, blackberry, catnip, chamomile, daisy, gardenia, grape, lettuce, morning glory, pansy, periwinkle, tansy, and tomato. Additionally, choose plants that thrive in a damp, watery environment, such as water lily.

Patterns

Very fluid patterns (no square or angular edges) so the garden flows like a wave are ideal.

Stones, Minerals, Crystals, and Shells

Use lots of seashells—the bigger, the better! Additionally, any stones that bear the colors of the sea or are aligned with the Water Element, including aquamarine, coral, holey stones, lapis, sodalite, and waterworn beach pebbles are good choices.

Colors

Sea green and blue are well-suited to this garden.

Decorative touches

A statue of a goddess standing on or backed by a large shell would be one idea. Alternatively, how about a castle carving to represent Oto's underwater dwelling place. Whatever you place here, make sure you include some water catchers and something like a fountain that has *moving* water, which represents Oto's life-giving power.

Direction

The magickal Quarter associated with Water is West. In feng shui the ebb and flow of life sits in the North, and time resides in the Southeast.

Adaptations

Within the house the art of aquarium gardens is experiencing a wonderful rebirth. Here, rather than housing fish, the aquarium tank becomes a garden of delightful underwater plants mingled with stones and shells to please even Oto's discerning eye. Most Web sites that are dedicated to aquarium care include information on water plants and their care.

After-Harvest Applications

Plants from Oto's garden are excellent for rituals and spells aimed at slow, steady progress. Just as water slowly wears away stone, so Oto's harvest can begin manifesting changes.

If you have a project to which you wish to bring longevity, bind a symbol of that project together with some dried plants from Oto's garden. Make sure the bundle is visually pretty, as this pleases the goddess. Keep this someplace where it will not be disturbed to protect your efforts over the long-haul. In particular keeping it near your fireplace or stove is a good idea, because the flame here represents constancy.

Pali Kongju: Shamanic Garden

Don't tell me about your visions unless they grow corn.
—*Sun Bear*

Histo-Cultural Information

In Korean stories, Pali Kongju was the first of all shamans. It is her blood that runs in each shaman's veins. The tale begins with Pali's father, who did not want another female child. He tossed her to the seas, where golden turtles rescued the goddess and brought her to shore to live with simple peasants. From the moment Pali Kongju arrived, the peasant couple and Pali experienced improved fortune.

When she grew older, a desperate duty fell upon Pali Kongju: that of fetching medicine water from the West to heal her birth parents. It did not please Pali, but she felt she had to go. She donned iron shoes and took up an iron staff and began to travel. Her journey took her by the Northern and Southern Stars and past the farming mistress and laundress of heaven, both of whom made her do chores before proceeding further!

Finally Pali Kongju reached the Western shore and met the god who protected the healing waters. This god asked her to marry him and bear him seven sons before he would release the water into her keeping. Sadly, by the time she returned home, her birth parents had already died. Nonetheless, she sprinkled the sacred waters on their bodies and they returned miraculously to life. Needless to say, Pali Kongju's parents were exceedingly grateful and proud—and saddened by the way they treated her at birth. Rather than try to keep her near, they wished her well and blessed her return to the otherworld where she could continue to help those in need. Pali Kongju's magickal attributes include healing, life, vitality, incantations, inspiration, Shamanic arts, and service to others.

Plants

All healthful plants are sacred to this goddess. Examples common in Shamanic traditions include alfalfa, aloe, aspen, beech, birch, black-eyed Susan, cabbage, catnip, celery seed, chicory, dandelion, juniper, mint, nettle, onion, parsley, pumpkin, raspberry, sage, strawberry, sunflower, thyme, and willow.

Patterns

Anything with a seven-point motif (to represent Pali Kongju's seven sons) is one option. Alternatively the outline of a turtle done with gold-painted stones would be apt.

Stones, Minerals, Crystals, and Shells

Seashells are ideal.

Colors

Gold and yellow tones are appropriate for this garden.

Decorative Touches

Anything that holds water, to represent the container in which the goddess bore her healing draught back to her parents, is suitable. Alternatively, add an ornate box (which, according to lore, protected her from the sea until the turtles found her) to your garden.

Direction

Pali Kongju returned to her home in the West, which is also the magickal region of Water so it's quite appropriate. In Shamanism this direction is also where the Ancestors traditionally reside. Feng shui sees things a little differently, putting Pali Kongju's healing attributes in the East and her gentle service in the Northwest.

Adaptations

Returning to the idea of a decorative box, look for something that's hinged (with a lid) but large enough to house whatever plants you've chosen. Put this in a West-facing window to invoke Pali Kongju's blessings.

After-Harvest Applications

Use the plants grown in your garden in charms, spells, and rituals aimed at awakening your own healing gifts or improving Shamanic awareness of self, Earth, and tribe. I make mine into an anointing oil that I dab on my chakaras before doing energy work for anyone else. This helps attune me to Pali Kongju's healing energies, the person with whom I'm working, and the Sacred for improved results.

Psyche: Butterfly Garden

The butterfly counts not months
but moments, and has time enough.
—*Rabindranath Tagore*

Histo-Cultural Information

In the Greek language Psyche's name means soul, and the butterfly has long been a symbol for this powerful spiritual aspect in humans. As the legend goes, Psyche lived alone by day and made love with her husband only in the dark, never seeing him. Year after year this continued until finally Psyche could not restrain her curiosity and brought a lantern into her bedroom. The glow revealed the body of the handsome, winged Eos, who instantly flew away. The moral of this story, in the eyes of the Greeks, was that romantic love only remains until reality comes to bear on the relationship.

Psyche was mortified by what happened and committed herself to numerous tasks to regain her love. Among them was sorting seeds, claiming the sun-sheep's fleece, and even going to the underworld to get beautifying ointment. Eventually this effort reunited her with Eos in heaven, with whom she bore the children Love and Delight. In this manner, like the butterfly transformed, the diligence of the soul found eternal happiness.

Psyche's magickal attritbutes include self-awareness, transformation, diligence, duty, devotion, and steadfastness.

Plants

For this garden we turn to plants known to attract butterflies. In particular, choose flowers that are composite-shaped (such as daisy), that have clusters of petals on one stem, or that have flat tops. These all make good landing fields for your winged guests. Additionally, strong aromatics and flowers that produce plentiful nectar (such as bee balm, black-eyed Susan, butterfly bush, coneflower, and zinnia) are appropriate.

To attract moths instead you'll want to turn to night-blooming flowers, such as night-blooming jasmine and four o'clock. Additionally, a successful butterfly garden requires plenty of sunshine, wind breaks, a location safe from predators, and water sources.

To feed caterpillars you'll require host plants, where butterflies will lay their eggs. Choices here include hollyhock, dill, clover, parsley, and milkweed.

Patterns

A butterfly is, of course, ideal!

Stones, Minerals, Crystals, and Shells

I suggest something such as clear quartz, which bears a resemblance to the clear chrysalis cocoon for monarch butterflies.

Colors

Studies show that butterflies seem to be attracted to orange, yellow, and purple flowers.

Decorative Touches

A statue of Eos, butterfly-shaped garden stakes, and water catchers or fountains are all good choices.

Direction

The energy of transformation seems to place this garden in the Eastern Quarter in both magick and feng shui. This direction stimulates, inspires, and provides winds upon which one's soul (or the butterflies) may fly!

Adaptations

Butterfly gardens can't be done indoors, but a nice symbolic alternative would be putting a wind chime with butterflies on it in an East-facing window. Beneath this you could grow a plant known to attract butterflies to attract Psyche's energy.

After-Harvest Applications

Magick is to bend and change, and Psyche is an ideal goddess to teach us this lesson. When you require more transformative or adaptive power, use the components from her garden to support your magickal efforts. In particular, the aromatic flowers would be ideal to make into incense or potpourri for meditative purposes, especially meditations aimed at integrating and accepting change gracefully.

Rati: Garden of Pleasures

> All the things I really like to do are
> either immoral, illegal, or fattening.
> —*Alexander Woollcott*

Histo-Cultural Information

What would life be without pleasure? Be it the warm welcome of sunshine on your face after a long winter or a sensual exchange with a lover, pleasure is a necessity to healthy human living. To help bring more pleasure into our lives, or to release our sense of self consciousness, we turn to Rati for assistance.

In Hindu tradition Rati was the passionate wife of the love god Kama. In her stories Rati is fruitful and giving. Though her energy often embodied sexual encounters, she also symbolized the pleasure of enlightenment coming to fruition in the human soul.

Rati's magickal attributes include magickal arts, sensuality, pleasure, happiness, fulfillment, and enlightenment

Plants

As one might expect, Rati's garden is filled with plants that somehow inspire happiness and bliss. To discover this state with a man, sow gardenia, jasmine, or lavender. To discover it with a woman, sow patchouli, vetivert, and violet. For overall energy with one's bed partner, sow beans, cohosh, ferns, heather, and pansy.

Patterns

This is a personal choice. What pattern does your pleasure take? From where do you derive great joy? Use that imagery in this garden to attract Rati's attentions.

Stones, Minerals, Crystals, and Shells

To build an air of beauty in the garden use amber, cat's-eye, and jasper. For overall happiness use amethyst. For passion use carnelian.

Colors

Pink and red are generally regarded as highly passionate colors, but if you have another hue that wakes up your pleasure-center, by all means use it.

Decorative Touches

Think bawdy—as a Victorian bedroom might appear if it had been set up outdoors! A statue of lovers entwined in an embrace might be ideal.

Direction

Magickally speaking, passion is a Fire-oriented energy and comes to us from the South. In feng shui, however, stimulation comes from the East.

Adaptations

Find a really sexy planter and fill it with an aromatic plant that you find personally pleasing (or one that arouses your mate). Keep this in the bedroom.

After-Harvest Applications

Jasmine, lavender, heather, and pansy are all edible flowers. Decant a handful of each in a liter of vodka, steeping until the petals turn translucent. Strain and add one cup of water, in which a half-cup of honey has been dissolved. Sip this expectantly with your significant other and take great pleasure in your time together!

Rhiannon: Summerland Garden

As a well-spent day brings happy sleep,
so a life well spent brings happy death.
— *Leonardo da Vinci*

Histo-Cultural Information

As the saying goes, nothing lasts forever. Humans face mortality issues every day, and not always as wisely and gracefully as we might wish. No matter how deep our faith, death is a difficult crossroad with which to cope, especially when it hits close to home. The idea behind creating a summerland garden is to honor death in a new way: as a part of life's wheel. In this lovely place you will find space to express your feelings about those who have passed over and to commemorate everything those individuals represent.

I've chosen Rhiannon for this garden because in Wales she is an underworld goddess who wakes the dead as she rides the summerland on her horse, accompanied by birds. Rhiannon never tires of riding, nor of her duties, which she undertakes joyfully. Some believe her white horse is a symbol of the moon. Her name translates as "great queen" (in this case presiding over the land of spirits). In this case we will call upon her birds to gently sing to those souls whose presence we miss and allow them to periodically come visit in our garden.

Rhiannon's magickal attributes include death, cycles, joy, travel, and lunar energy.

Plants

Funerary plants and herbs are appropriate, including basil, anaconite, periwinkle, violet, and yew. In addition to this, be sure to include any plants of which the deceased was (or were) particularly fond.

Patterns

A summerland garden might be patterned after a wheel or an outward-moving spiral to represent life's ongoing movement and the immortal nature of the human soul. Because you will be honoring the spirits of the departed here, it also encourages their progression in the next incarnation.

Stones, Minerals, Crystals, and Shells

Jet was the traditional Victorian stone of mourning. Obsidian is also appropriate, as it will collect sadness and negativity to itself and ground those feelings out as needed.

Colors

Contrary to mourning, the colors of this garden should be cheerful and bright. The idea is to celebrate the life and memories of this person or persons.

Decorative Touches

To welcome Rhiannon place statues of a galloping horse or birds on wing in the garden. Adjacent to these put images of the person or people that the garden commemorates. (Make sure to have a housing for the images that's weatherproof.)

Direction

Because we return to the earth upon our death, the magickal Quarter is North. That having been said, I might consider Northeast even more appropriate, because the wheel of time and life continues to move forward. Shamanism places the ancestors in the West, and feng shui puts family in the East and recognition/honor in the South.

Adaptations

Within the house a horse- or bird-shaped planter filled with violets might be a nice touch on your altar, along with images of the person or people you wish to hold close to heart and mind.

After-Harvest Applications

The summerland garden can symbolically help you with any type of ending, not just a physical one. What cycles in your life do you wish would stop? What relationships are no longer healthy? Use Rhiannon's harvest as spell and ritual components to help you cope effectively with these kinds of issues and achieve closure.

Saga: Divination Garden

Let it be discovered by divination.
—Hittite prayer

Histo-Cultural Information

In Teutonic tradition Saga is a faithful attendant of Frigg, whose name means seeress or all-knowing one. Some historians believe it is more likely that Saga was actually an aspect of Frigg whose position altered with history and bardic tradition. According to the sacred writings of the Eddas, Saga lived at Sinking Beach, which was a waterfall where she offered all her guests a drink from a golden cup. Saga is a teacher, but she is also a student of the Universe. She is often depicted with a long Viking braid, an emblem of womanhood and honor. Later, her name was applied to the sacred heroic texts of the Scandanavian people.

With this in mind, it seems appropriate to use Saga as the energy signature around which to form one's visionary garden. Not only can Saga provide us with divinatory ability, but also the capacity to communicate what we see in an effective, constructive manner!

Saga's magickal attributes include future-telling, fate, creativity, learning, wisdom, womanhood, devotion, and priestess energy.

Plants

Any plant that has been used for divinatory arts will please this goddess. Included in this list we find bay, bean, broom, cherry, dandelion, fig, grape, marigold, meadowsweet, mint, oak, rowan, and yarrow, just to name a few.

Patterns

The Teutons associated Saga with the astrological sign of Pisces, so the image of a fish or a pair of fish is one good possibility. (It's not difficult to turn the line drawing for Pisces into a garden outline as the following depicts.)

Another appropriate shape would be that of an open eye.

Stones, Minerals, Crystals & Shells

Make a bed of crystals and stones (as drainage) for your garden out of rocks that support psychic awareness. Options include amethyst, aquamarine, azurite, beryl, quartz, lapis, citrine, hematite, jet, moonstone, and tigereye.

Colors

Traditionally, divination is associated with the color yellow.

Decorative Touches

You could get really creative here. For example, have a reflective ball as the center point (looking much like a scrying stone). You could also enclose some tarot cards in protective covering and plant them around the edges of the garden so they look to be growing out of the border work.

Direction

Magickally speaking, divination often resides in the East with the Wind, as the ancient oracles in Greece often used the wind as the bearer of divine missives. In feng shui I'd opt for the Northwest, the center of service to others.

Adaptations

Keep a planter filled with Saga's greenery in the room where you enact any divinatory process to inspire accuracy and improved insights. I recently even found a planter shaped like the astrological sign of Pisces!

After-Harvest Applications

Watching your garden's messages in itself can be quite an experience. Because you've invited Saga to live among the flowers, don't be surprised if you start getting messages from those plants long before harvesting. Divination by natural omens and signs is among the oldest arts for seers!

You can bundle any of the flowers and plants from Saga's garden into a pendulum structure and use them as tools. Alternatively, dry and burn the items and observe the behavior of the flame for interpretive values. If you need a good book that discusses how to interpret different divination methods, try *FutureTelling* (Crossing Press).

Tara: Garden of Beauty

A beautiful thing is never perfect.
—*Egyptian Proverb*

Histo-Cultural Information

Our world is a very superficial place sometimes, yet what would life be without some semblance of true beauty therein? The key here is not focusing so much on cursory details and thus missing the loveliness of simplicity and inner comeliness. Tara is the ideal goddess to help us see those wonderful things that we all too often miss.

Tara comes to us from Hindu lore as having been born from Avalokitesvara's tears. (He oversees all matters of compassion and "light.") It is no wonder, then, that she is represented as a beautiful burning star—burning with desire to grow, to change, to transform even as the human spirit and soul. The attributes of self control, spiritual mastery, and mystical proficiency are under her guidance. Her name means she who delivers or star, both of which indicate a kind of guidance to those of us who have lost site of our true self.

Tara's magickal attributes include Sun and Moon Magick, beauty, attractiveness, compassion, overcoming, and protection.

Plants

If you can have 21 varieties of plants in the garden, that's Tara's number, because 21 forms of her have been discovered. Some of the flowers and herbs you might want to include are those known to promote beauty, including avocado, catnip, maidenhair, and heather. Beyond this, gather dew on May Day and transfer it into your garden. This water is said to have strong magickal abilities to make anything more lovely.

Patterns

A star or a boat (the vessel in which she ferry's people from a chaotic world into one that has order and beauty) is suitable. Motifs with three sides or shapes are also a good choice, as Tara has three eyes.

Stones, Minerals, Crystals, and Shells

Above and beyond any stones that have strong visual appeal, look to those crystals whose energy matrix accents attractiveness such as amber, cat's-eye and jasper.

Colors

Green and white are most common but blue and red are also found in Tara's artistic depictions. Note that white often appears on Tara's left side in the form of a lotus, meaning that white flowers might be best put on the left side of your garden. In particular I favor the silver fern for this garden because it reminds me of the silvery-white color of the moon and stars.

Decorative Touches

Use 108 border stones for Tara's garden, as 108 is the number of prayer beads used to invoke her sacred names. Also, playful items are excellent touches for this garden because Tara is often shown as a mischievous youth.

Besides these, Hindu art portrays her with a sun in one hand and accompanied by a lion, so these two images would be appropriate accents.

Direction

Magickally speaking, beauty is everywhere! To try to limit this attribute to one direction or type of energy would be a terrible disservice to Nature. In feng shui, Tara's region might be West, because that is where the color of white/silver abides along with an inner harmony that is, itself, wholly beautiful.

Adaptations

The best place in the house for a Tara planter is next to the mirror where you do most of your primping and fussing. I suggest using a fragrant indoor flower so that the aroma subtly encourages self-confidence and less superficial hangups.

After-Harvest Applications

I use Tara's plants in oils and bath soaks when I need to look and feel my best. Let's face it: There are days when we get up, look in the mirror, and think *yuck!* This is the ideal time to ask Tara for an attitude adjustment! For example, take a little heather oil and dab it on your heart chakra while saying:

> I AM BEAUTIFUL WITHIN AND WITHOUT;
> TARA REMOVE LINGERING SELF DOUBTS!

Tatsuta-Hime: Garden of the Winds

Hoist your sail when the wind is fair.
—*Proverb*

Histo-Cultural Information

Nothing is as invigorating and inspiring as standing and facing a gentle Spring wind. The sensation is cool, stimulating, and yet welcoming. In many ancient traditions the wind is also associated with spirits, because even though you know the wind is there, you cannot see it! Magickally speaking the wind is associated with movement, change, motivation, and life's breath.

To create our wind garden we look to Tatsuta-Hime, a goddess from Japan. Each fall this lady would don a kaleidesope-colored tapestry as diverse in hue as the Autumn leaves. Then she would magickally transform into the wind, merrily scattering those leaves to the four corners of creation!

Tatsuta-Hime's magickal attributes include the harvest, travel safety especially for sailing, fishing luck, and Wind and Air Magick.

Plants

Any item that has long, supple leaves or flowers to dance in the wind is one option. Alternatively, look to plants that are associated with the Air Element, such as bean, bergamot, broom, borage, clover, dandelion, eyebright, goldenrod, lavender, marjoram, pine, sage, and verbena.

Patterns

A leaf pattern is one choice. Beyond that, let your whimsy run wild and free as the wind itself (which usually doesn't like to be constrained anyway).

Stones, Minerals, Crystals, and Shells

Stones associated with Air include adventurine, jasper, mica, pumice, and sphene.

Colors

Choose pastels for this garden.

Decorative Touches

Place wind chimes, flags, and anything that will catch the winds (so you can enjoy them better) everywhere!

Direction

Magickally, the Air Element resides in the East, bringing renewed hope with each breeze. This seems to harmonize nicely with feng shui, which places the attributes of beginnings and awakening in this region.

Adaptations

My indoor wind garden is a simple planter placed beneath a favorite wind chime. Note, however, that I looked for a chime that had russets and orange to honor the Fall and this goddess's colors.

After-Harvest Applications

The best time to harvest the wind garden is the Fall, which is Tatsuta-Hime's season. Afterward release the harvest to various directional winds with your wishes. Use a Southerly wind for wishes associated with love and relationships, a Westerly wind for healing and intuition, a Northerly wind for money and foundations, and an Easterly wind for the conscious mind and learning.

Venus: Garden of Love

A heart that loves is always young.
—*Greek Proverb*

Histo-Cultural Information

If love makes the world go round, then tis' Venus that puts a spin on the whole relationship equation! As the Roman equivalent to Aphrodite, this goddess embodied amazing charm, the compassion of a mother, the sensual energy of a new bride, and the wisdom of a crone in relationship matters.

With this in mind, asking Venus for her help in creating a garden of love seems natural. Try to leave a space in this garden where you and your significant other can sit together, literally surrounded by loving energies.

Venus's magickal attributes include fruitfulness, sensuality, love, devotion, sagacity, and family and kin.

Plants

Plan your Venus garden in Spring, which is her season. Some of the plants sacred to Venus include clover, cypress, love-oriented herbs, myrtle, pine, rose, strawberry, and sunflower.

Patterns

Lips, a heart, or the astrological symbol for the planet Venus all have potential.

Stones, Minerals, Crystals, and Shells

Stones preferred by Venus include cat's-eye, topaz, turquoise and any stone that inspires love (including self-love) such as pink quartz.

Colors

Pink, red, and purple are the predominant colors for love.

Decorative Touches

Images of sparrows, doves, bulls, lions, and lynx are all sacred to Venus. Additionally, because her imagery often overlaps Aphrodite, you could get a statue of a goddess standing on a seashell.

Direction

Love's magickal center is due South, where the energy of fire can keep the warmth and passion alive. Its feng shui direction varies according to the focus: Family is due East, and general relationships reside in the Southwest.

Adaptations

Aloe, marjoram, parsley, and tea rose all come under Venus's dominion and are ideal indoor plants. Find a container that's a deep red or reddish-purple color or one shaped like a heart for best results. Keep this in a room where you spend the most time with loved ones.

After-Harvest Applications

The best dates to use anything from your Venus garden are those during which she was customarily venerated (a word, by the way, that takes its root from her name). These dates include March 10; April 1, 14, 21, 23, 28; May 3; June 24; July 19; August 19; and October 9. Also, any Friday is appropriate. Remember that although Venus's components are certainly geared toward love, use them cautiously. Don't try to manipulate another's heart. Instead, simply welcome the energy of love into your life and watch the wonders it works.

Vila: Garden of Healing

Health is the greatest gift,
contentment the greatest wealth,
faithfulness the best relationship.
—*Buddha*

Histo-Cultural Information

Every mother I know stresses the importance of health to a person's overall well-being. One cannot have a healthy mind and spirit without also having a healthy body. These three aspects intertwine in the human trinity for balance, a long life, happiness, and magick!

To help us in the task of remaining healthy or returning to wholeness, this garden is dedicated to Vila. She comes to us from Eastern Europe, where she was among the most powerful goddesses. Her imagery is lovely, complete with gentle wings and golden hair. Stories also show her diligently watching over woodland creatures and making sure the land gets enough rain.

More importantly to this particular garden, however, is Vila's talent with healing plants and rituals. Those people who please her will be able to learn her arts, and her secrets.

Vila's magickal attributes include Nature (forests), weather magick, herbal arts, and healing and health.

Plants

Any plant commonly used in herbalism for healing or maintaining health is perfect for Vila's gardens and groves. Included in this list are angelica, balm, carnation, cucumber, fennel, gardenia, garlic, geranium, hop, juniper, marjoram, mint, onion, rose, sassafras, tansy, thyme, vervain, and violet.

Patterns

The pattern of a rainbow is a good choice for Vila, who was born of rainbows and mists. Any image that you associate with health and wholeness (such as a circle or a predominantly red cross) is appropriate as well.

Stones, Minerals, Crystals, and Shells

Look to stones that were carried as healthful amulets, such as agate, amber, amethyst, bloodstone, carnelian, coral, quartz, hematite, jet, lapis, obsidian, sodalite, and turquoise.

Colors

Light green has strong associations with healing. (This color is frequently part of visualization for auric cleansing and balancing.)

Decorative Touches

Vila was known to shapeshift into a falcon, horse, snake, swan, or whirlwind—the latter of which might be portrayed as a spiral made from rocks.

Direction

Most often health is considered an aspect of Water (that is, West) but more dramatic problems might require Fire (South). The direction in which health resides in feng shui is due East.

Adaptations

The nicest indoor application for Vila's planters is making them for people who are ailing. Even up to 100 years ago flowers were thought to lift the spirits of sickly people and speed recovery.

After-Harvest Applications

Always harvest Vila's garden at sunrise on a Sunday during the full moon. If you can't combine these three factors, do your best to achieve two. Draw a circle in the dirt around the plant you wish to harvest using a birch twig or broom handle. Leave an offering there for the plant spirit and Vila, whisper your need to her, and then take only what you need of the plant for your spellcraft, potions, or rituals.

White Buffalo Woman: Ritual Garden

Form follows function—that has been misunderstood.
Form and function should be one, joined in a spiritual union.
—*Frank Lloyd Wright*

Histo-Cultural Information

It has been said that the groves were the gods' first temples. This garden is a makeshift outdoor temple for worship and magickal workings with a little help from White Buffalo Woman.

As the story goes, aeons ago White Buffalo Woman brought important information to humans. Her first encounter was with two young men. One desired her and the other honored her apparent power. The first lost his life, and the second helped his village create a sacred space in which White Buffalo Woman imparted the secrets of the pipe and all the rituals that accompanied such a sacred item.

She also gently reminded the people to honor the Earth and always live in harmony with it. Her words were well-spoken and well-received. When her teachings were completed, she turned into a white buffalo and walked out of the village as mysteriously as she came.

White Buffalo Woman's magickal attributes include ecology, environmentalism, Earth Magick, ritual work and tools, and Shamanism.

Plants

There are so many plants that have found their way into ritual that it's nearly impossible to list them all. However, following Shamanic tradition, cedar, lavender, and sage are three good choices that are used to purify the sacred space.

Patterns

A motif of seven parts or points, because White Buffalo Woman walked seven times around the ritual fire as she taught, is a good choice. Note: If you follow this motif, make sure to have a centralized fire source for the garden.

Also note that the layout of your garden should reflect the kind of space you traditionally use for ritual (most of us use a circle), but if there's another form or pattern you follow, integrate it into your garden somehow.

Stones, Minerals, Crystals, and Shells

Found stones are best, as the Native Americans often saw these as a message from Nature spirits or the gods.

Colors

White is the ideal color to use in this garden.

Decorative Touches

Porcupine and buffalo are her sacred animals. (She appeared in a porcupine cloak to the two men she met). Alternatively, some type of medicine wheel or ritual pipe would be very fitting.

Direction

As a goddess/ancestor spirit, White Buffalo Woman resides in the West from a Shamanic point of view. Magickally her space is "center," as that is where magick begins. Alternatively you could see her as the circle's circumference.

Adaptations

The greatest honor you can give White Buffalo Woman is to treat your entire living area as a sacred space in which she is welcome. Enact ritual in every room of the house, and recognize that the Great Spirit is part of all things in waking and sleeping, in sounds and silences. This makes life an act of worship and a very real ritual that commemorates White Buffalo Woman's messages!

After-Harvest Applications

Dry the herbs and flowers from White Buffalo Woman's garden and burn them prior to ritual to prepare your sacred space. Fan the herbs around the circle clockwise using a natural feather, which must be found as a gift from nature, *not* harvested in any manner, and properly cleansed. As you move through the space, you may want to add a special chant.

Yemaja: Zodiac Garden

Recently, someone asked me if I believed in astrology.
He seemed somewhat puzzled when I explained
that the reason I don't is that I'm a Gemini.
—*Raymond Smullyan*

Histo-Cultural Information

Yemaja is a goddess from Nigeria whose name means fish mother. Her mother being an earth goddess and sister of the sun god, her name in Brazilian tradition rings with rich importance.

At one point in her mythic cycle Yemaja bears eleven gods and goddesses along with streams of water from her breasts. Symbolically speaking the streams equate to the Milky Way, on which the eleven Beings reside along with Yemaja, who herself represents the astrological sign of Cancer (the crab).

Yemaja's magickal attributes include fertility, celestial harmony, energy, and any attribute related to the sign of Cancer (love of nature, enjoyment of socialization and public work, good memory, and sense of the "odds").

Plants

Plan your Yemaja garden on New Year's, the traditional festival day when she receives offerings. This might be an ideal time to place seeds on your altar and bless them, giving some back to the earth as a gift that honors the goddess. Beyond this, you'll want to gather at least one plant to represent each astrological sign. This can be done by Elemental correspondence, energy attributes, or direct association with the sign itself. See Part 1 for some ideas.

Patterns

The best type of layout for this garden is that of a circle in which the plants associated with each sign are laid out into 12 sections. Alternatively, use the outline of Cancer's astrological symbol to honor the goddess and welcome her in that space.

Stones, Minerals, Crystals, and Shells

Follow the pattern of birthstones around the astrological wheel. Specifically:

Aries	Bloodstone or garnet
Taurus	Jade or lapis
Gemini	Agate or aventurine
Cancer	Beryl or moonstone
Leo	Amber or carnelian
Virgo	Agate or aventurine
Libra	Lapis or turquoise
Scorpio	Tourmalated quartz
Sagittarius	Amethyst or sugilite
Capricorn	Hematite or onyx
Aquarius	Aquamarine or jet
Pisces	Amethyst or sugilite

Colors

Blue, which is said to be Yemaja's favorite color, is ideal.

Decorative Touches

A mermaid, which is how art often depicts Yemaja, is a good choice. Also, a telescope might make a neat centerpiece if you can properly cover it.

Direction

Up. Seriously. Because the stars are up, that's my opinion. You might want to add a mirror to the center of the garden so you can easily see the stars in the center of the greenery at night.

Adaptations

Put a circular pot in a window where it can easily collect the light from evening stars.

After-Harvest Applications

The zodiac is a gentle reminder of life's wheel and time's motion. Let your garden's growth, life, death, and rebirth throughout the year keep this awareness in the forefront of your mind. When you're having trouble coping with or breaking a cycle, use the harvest from the garden in rituals and spells. Also, when you need to accent the energies of any one sign in your life, carry a cutting from that part of the garden with you for the day.

Zemyna:
Garden of Fertility

The mountains are fountains of men as well as
of rivers, of glaciers, of fertile soil. The great poets,
philosophers, prophets, able men whose thought
and deeds have moved the world, have come down
from the mountains.
—*John Muir*

Histo-Cultural Information

I can think of no goddess better suited to the task of clos-
ing out this section other than Zemyna. In Lithuanian stories,
this earth goddess was remembered and thanked for the gift of
life at every birth. Zemyna didn't just preside over human fertility, though. She was the life of Earth itself: Every flower,
tree, and weed was watched and cared for by this goddess, whose
name means flower-giver.

Zemnya's magickal attributes include fertility, Earth
Magick, plant spirits and plant lore, gardens, and groves.

Plants

In particular it's important to have at least one tree (even
a miniature one) in Zemyna's garden, because it is in the tree
tops that she hid the secret of life. Birch, linden, maple, oak,
and spruce are her preferred trees. Lilies were also loved by
this goddess, as that is where the spirits of young girls resided.
The ancestors lived among fruit bearing trees.

Patterns

A yoni symbol or an oval, both of which represent the gate of life through which all souls must pass, are good choices for this garden.

Stones, Minerals, Crystals, and Shells

Use any stones that were used as charms to improve physical fertility, including amber, geode (a womb-like shaped one is best), moonstone, and pearl. Alternatively, look for stones whose shapes represents the vagina and penis to meld male-female energy together, which results in "creative" power.

Colors

Yellow (pastel) is appropriate.

Decorative Touches

Images of young animals or children as well as a pregnant goddess statue are good choices.

Direction

Fertility is a function of the East and sometimes of the South in magick. (The East brings the power of creation; the South inspires passion.) In feng shui the Southeast Quadrant would seem to bear similar significance.

Adaptations

Inside the home I recommend using a yellow planter shaped like a pregnant goddess' belly or something similarly feminine. The ability to create new life is most definitely a yin quality. Add to this yellow flowers or any herb/plant known to inspire fertility. One option that combines both ideas is the daffodil. (Daffodil requires a planter deep enough for the bulb and roots.)

After-Harvest Applications

In looking at Zemyna's garden, remember that fertility need not mean just physical or procreative energy. One may have fertile ideas, abundant energy, or even a truly prolific garden! Apply Zemyna's harvest to these goals or simply enjoy her beauty, for hers is the Earth—the garden of the world, all of which is a lesson and a sacred space that we share.

Afterword

Our spiritual lives need not be kept separate from daily living. In fact, we can cultivate a healthier spirit through gardens and groves, landscaping and leisure hours where we enjoy our handiwork. Remember that the Divine is part of all things and that the energy of life buzzes in each bud and blossom, leaf and lawn (even those you have to mow!). To touch the Earth intimately is to know yourself and the God/dess better. I wish you many blessings in this adventure.

—February 2001

Appendix

Theme Gardening

Earlier in this book I discussed applying the ideas presented in Part II in theme gardens. For example, Venus's garden becomes simply a love or passion garden. This approach is especially useful for people who may feel a little uncomfortable with the religious aspect of goddess gardening (or for those who have magickally challenged neighbors!).

This appendix expands on this idea, specifically to illustrate several theme gardens that don't have goddess-oriented overtones. The types of gardens you can create is limited only by your imagination. Even those with magickal or spiritual themes have amazing potential for diversity. My hope is that this section will inspire many more ideas of your own.

Aromatherapy or Incense Garden

With holistics and homeopathy finding a strong foothold in our modern health practices, an aromatherapy garden is one way to create an atmosphere of well-being around your home. Better still, many of the items in an aromatherapy garden have scent-releasing flowers, and therefore it's visually pleasing as well!

Historical records indicate that the Egyptians used aromatics to treat melancholy, the Greeks considered aromatic herbs as a gift from the gods, Babylonians scented their temples with a variety of herbs and flowers, and lavender appears regularly in Medieval texts as a supportive aroma that helps the healing process along. Even Hippocrates advocated aromatics in his writings. I see no reason why we can't apply these ideas to our modern pursuit of wholeness within and without.

Some of the plants that appear in aromatherapy texts, along with their applications, are detailed in the following list.

Herb	Applications
Anise	Energy and protection
Bergamot	Anxiety and stress relief
Carnation	Health and vitality
Chamomile	Emotional balance and calmness
Clary	Communication
Coriander	Decreasing aggravation
Dill	Tension relief
Fennel	Overcoming blockage
Gardenia	Accord and health
Geranium	Balance and harmony
Honeysuckle	Prosperity
Hops	Restfulness
Hyacinth	Meditation and focus
Juniper	Easing aches and pains
Lavender	Insomnia, inner peace
Lilac	Psychic awareness
Magnolia	Spirituality
Marjoram	Decreasing worries
Mint	Refreshed energy, memory improvement

Pine	Cleansing and purification
Rose	Love (including self-love)
Geranium	Courage
Rosemary	Mental keenness (especially memory)
Sage	Clearing negative energy
Sweetpea	Strengthening friendship
Thyme	Improving personal wards
Violet	Self image

After you harvest your aromatherapy garden, carefully dry the leaves and flowers so you can use them in making incense and oils, for strewing around a sacred space, or as part of sachets that scent your entire wardrobe with healthy vibrations!

Sacred Circle Garden

In magickal traditions, it's common to create sacred space in the shape of a circle. This shape represents many things: the wheel of time; the wheel of life, death, and rebirth; the sphere where we step out of the mundane into the metaphysical and spiritual; a globe upon which all who stand are of equal importance in the greater scheme of things; and a protective boundary, keeping out negative energies and holding in magickal power until it's ready to be released and guided to its destination.

The traditional sacred circle is a kind of mandala that has four distinct parts and a central point. The Northern Quarter of the circle represents Earth, followed by the Air Element in the Eastern Quarter, Fire in the South, and Water in the West. These are the four components that create all energy, and the beings that reside within the Quarters are the Powers that watch over the sacred space.

How does this translate into gardening? For those with larger lawns, I envision a huge circular garden where one can hold ritual or cast spells. Even without that amount of land, the idea of having a permanent sacred space anywhere on one's property is really wonderful. It invokes the goddess and all of her magick into your home, into the land, and into your life every moment of every day!

To create this effect outdoors you'll first need to decide how wide you want your circle to be. Divide that measurement in half and cut a length of rope to that size plus enough to tie around a steak or stick. Put the stick where you want the center of the circle to be, and then stretch out the string and begin to mark the circle's perimeter with small rocks or by etching it in the dirt. Remember to move clockwise as you do this to attract the most beneficial energy possible.

Using a compass, figure out where due North is and mark that location. From that spot, you can divide the circle into four equal Quarters that are aligned correctly to the cardinal points of the compass. At this juncture I place an energized, blessed coin in each of the four Quarters. (I actually use a quarter because of the symbolic value.) If these coins ever work to the surface of the soil, you'll know it's time to reinforce the energy in the soil and surrounding area.

Next, begin sowing the garden using each plant's Elemental correspondence. To give some examples, the North/Earth section might be bordered in fern, have a center of tulips and honeysuckle, and be filled in with honesty. The East/Air section might be bordered with mint or parsley and filled out with lavender and lily of the valley. The South/Fire section can be bordered in thistle and snapdragon, centered around sunflower, and filled in with marigold. Finally the West/Water section might be bordered with thyme or tansy, centered around daffodil, and filled out with heather, periwinkle, and tea rose.

As you finish planting each Quarter, it's nice to add an invocation to the Element of that Quarter. An invocation "invites" the energy into that space. Here is an example for each Quarter:

- ◆ **North/Earth:** Hail and welcome guardians of the Earth see here the work of my hands and be pleased. Bless this soil and all that grows herein to be filled with your energy for nurturing, for firm foundations, for prosperity. So be it.

- ◆ **East/Air:** Hail and welcome guardians of the Air see here the work of my hands and be pleased. Bless this soil and all that grows herein to be filled with your energy for inspiration, communication, motivation, and fresh outlooks. So be it.

- ◆ **South/Fire:** Hail and welcome guardians of the Fire see here the work of my hands and be pleased. Bless this soil and all that grows herein to be filled with your energy for passion, power, purification, and illumination. So be it.

- ◆ **West/Water:** Hail and welcome guardians of the Water see here the work of my hands and be pleased. Bless this soil and all that grows herein to be filled with your energy for healing, creativity, cleansing, and endurance. So be it.

Adapting the sacred circle garden to indoor efforts might be best accomplished by four separate containers, each of which would be placed in the appropriate part of your home. Check the amount of light and space you have available so you can choose the plants that will fit these criteria. Next, find Elementally colored containers into which to put your chosen flora. For Earth, use green or brown; for Air, yellow or white; for Fire, red or orange; and for Water, blue or purple.

Alternatively, find containers that have imagery that promotes each Element. For example, finding a crock with a wave pattern upon it would be ideal for Water and Water-associated plants. Note: You can still put a blessed coin in the bottom of each as with the outdoor version.

After the harvest, carefully mark from which part of the garden each item came. This way you always have Elemental components to use in your magick.

Wish Garden

Wishcraft is a very ancient and simple form of magick based in sympathy and symbolism. A good example comes to us in weather spells. When someone wished for rain, he or she would dip a broom or bundle of herbs in water and then sprinkle it out on the ground (showing the clouds what to do). These types of mini-spells exist around the world, and there are some growable components that have traditionally been used to affect results in wishcraft. Here's a brief list with their applied energies:

Plant	Wishing Application
Amaranth	Divine favor
Angelica	Blessings and health
Basil	Happiness
Bean	Prophetic dreams
Carrot	Joy and luck
Chrysanthemum	Congeniality and hospitality
Clover	Luck (esp. 4 leaf variety)
Daisy	Love
Dandelion	Manifestation
Evergreen	Health and sustenance
Fern (flowering)	Treasure
Flower (the one associated with your birth month)	Fulfillment

Flower, red	Divine favor
Gooseberry	Wisdom
Holly	Manifestation
Lavender	Wish fulfillment
Lilac (five-petal)	Luck
Marjoram	Wealth
Onion	Luck
Potato, new	Wish fulfillment
Rose	Wish expression (to divine)
Sage	Dream manifestation
Sunflower	Simple wishes
Tomato	Prosperity
Violet	Wishes of the heart

If you have other growable items that you associate with specific forms of wishing, by all means add them to this list and sow them in your garden!

You can pattern the garden in any way that's personally pleasing, but it might be neat to add a wishing well to the center where you can drop a coin or two, as is still the tradition. This supports the wishcraft being established in that area. When the well gets filled, donate the coins to a good cause to spread the blessings!

As you harvest the various items, the ways you can apply them to wishcraft are pretty diverse. Float them on waters so your wish goes out to the seas and beyond. Scatter them to the winds so the air and birds can carry the wish further. Burn them so the smoke rises to the heavens with your wish, or bury them back in the soil so wishes grow into manifested form!

God Garden

I included this theme garden for those of you who read this book and thought, *What about the other side of the coin?* The Sacred Parent is neither male nor female alone; rather, it is both and neither. The Goddess offers much to our technological, right-brained world, but the God and masculine aspects should not be overlooked. In particular He offers strength, stamina, energy, leadership, vitality, logic, sound judgement, an authoritative demeanor, warrior energy in times of need, protection, and the ability to "hunt" successfully.

Some of the plants associated with the God aspect include:

Plant	Deity
Apple	Dionysus, Apollo, Zeus
Ash	Woden, Thor, Neptune, Mars
Basil	Vishnu
Bay	Apollo
Birch	Thor
Broccoli	Jupiter
Carnation	Jupiter
Cypress	Mithras, Pluto, Cupid, Jupiter
Daisy	Thor
Dill	Horus
Elm	Odin
Fennel	Dionysus
Fern	Puck
Fig	Dionysus
Gorse	Thor
Grape	Bacchus

Hazel	Mercury, Thor
Ivy	Osiris
Lavender	Saturn
Lily of the valley	Apollo
Mint	Pluto
Mullein	Jupiter
Mustard	Aesculapius
Narcissus	Hades
Nettle	Thor
Oak	Dagda, Jupiter, Thor, Pan
Orchid	Cronos
Orris	Osiris
Peony	Pan
Pepper	Ares
Pine	Pan, Attis, Dionysus
Poppy	Hypnos
Rose	Eros, Cupid, Adonis
Rowan	Thor
Saint-John's-wort	Baldur
Sesame	Ganesha
Tansy	Ganymede
Thistle	Thor
Vervain	Mars, Jupiter, Thor
Willow	Mercury, Belinus

Some type of phallic symbol would be appropriate as an outline for the god garden (bear in mind that it need not be overt if you have nosy or puritanical neighbors). Similarly, any stones with points are considered having masculine symbolism. Finding statues shouldn't be difficult; I've seen stone pieces that depict specific deities (such as Zeus or Mercury) and others that show men doing various tasks that might represent a specific god's area of protection.

Plan and work your god garden during bright, daylight hours, as these support the conscious mind. As you reap from your garden, blend its harvest into your spells and rituals for your patron gods, those that focus on attracting traditional masculine attributes into your life or those for rites of passage for men.

Ghost Garden

A ghost garden is a really fun addition for families who like to celebrate Halloween in a boo-tiful way! For your center-piece, of course, you'll need a headstone. Put whatever message you want on it (or have several with messages you can change to suit the occasion).

To keep the nasty ghosts away, plant pumpkin around the garden and carve these at the appropriate times of the year Lammas and Hallows come immediately to mind. Other good deterrents for those mischievous types are juniper and some iron planted in the soil near the perimeter of your magickal space.

Traditionally ghosts were communed with or called upon in the safe haven of a sacred circle, so a circle is an ideal shape for either an indoor or outdoor ghost garden effort. As far as what to sow, look to:

- ♦ Angelica. To attract spirit guides and helpers specifically.
- ♦ Althea. To attract positive spirits and increase psychic awareness.
- ♦ Catnip. Harvest and hang it over the door to welcome friendly ghosts.

- Dandelion. To encourage ghostly visitations in dreams.
- Elder. Stand beneath this at midnight to encounter spirits.
- Gardenia. To promote peace between humans and spirits.
- Heather. To help to conjure ghosts.
- Lavender. To be able to see ghosts when they arrive.
- Marigold. Sprinkle petals on the walkway to your home to guide a child's spirit home.
- Mint. To attract kindly spirits (often ancestral).
- Sweetgrass. Dry, bundle, and burn to call on beneficient ghosts and spirits.
- Thistle. Harvest and place in hot water. The rising steam attracts positive spirits.
- Willow. Burn dried bark as part of conjuring rituals.

There will be specific times of the year when your ghost garden may see more use than others, such as New Year's, when the veil between worlds is said to grow thin. The spirits of family members often try to find their way home during holidays, so leave a picture of your ancestors in the garden with a small offering of favorite foods.

On those occasions when you're holding a ritual to contact spirits, toss some freshly gathered leaves and flowers from your garden near the doorway of your house as a sign of welcome. Remember, however, to set up a protected sacred space for any such undertaking or you may get more than for which you hoped!

Select Bibliography

Ann, Martha and Dorothy Meyers Imel. *Goddesses in World Mythology*. New York: Oxford University Press, 1993.

Beyerl, Paul. *Herbal Magick*. Custer, Wash.: Phoenix Publishing, 1998.

Black, George. *Folk Medicine*. New York: Burt Franklin Co., 1993.

Bruce-Mitford, Miranda. *Illustrated Book of Signs and Symbols*. New York: DK Publishing, 1996.

Clarkson, R.E. *Herbs and Savory Seeds*. New York: Dover Publications, 1972.

Clarkson, Rosetta. *Golden Age of Herbs and Herbalists*. New York: Dover Publications, 1940.

Cunningham, S. *Cunningham's Encyclopedia of Magical Herbs*. St. Paul, Minn.: Llewellyn Publications, 1985.

Dyer, T.F. *Folklore of Plants*. New York: D. Appleton & Co., 1889.

Farrar, Janet and Stewart. *Witch's Goddess*. Custer, Wash.: Phoenix Publishing, 1987.

Fox, Dr. William. *Family Botanical Guide.* Buffalo, N.Y.: JW Clement Co., 1935.

Freethy, Ron. *Book of Plant Uses, Names & Folklores.* New York: Tanager Books, 1985.

Gordon, Lesley. *Green Magic.* New York: Viking Press, 1972.

Gordon, Stuart. *Encyclopedia of Myths and Legends.* London: Headline Book Publishing, 1993.

Griggs, B. *History of Herbal Medicine.* New York: Viking Press, 1981.

Hall, Manly P. *Secret Teachings of All Ages.* Los Angeles: Philosophical Research Society, 1977.

Hyton, W. H. (Ed.) *Rodale's Illustrated Encyclopedia of Herbs.* Emmaus, Penn.: Rodale Press, 1987.

Kieckhefer, R. *Magic in the Middle Ages.* New York: Viking Press, 1980.

LeStrainge, R. *History of Herbal Plants.* New York: Arco Publishing, 1977.

Lurker, Manfred. *Dictionary of Gods and Goddesses, Devils and Demons.* New York: Routeledge & Kegan Paul Ltd., 1987.

MacNicol, Mary. *Flower Cookery.* New York: Fleet Press Corporation, 1967.

McLean, T. *Medieval English Gardens.* New York: Viking Press, 1980.

Monaghan, Patricia. *Book of Goddesses & Heroines.* St. Paul, Minn.: Llewellyn Publications, 1993.

Northcote, Lady Rosaline. *Book of Herb Lore*. New York: Dover Publications, 1912.

Potterton, D. (Ed.) Culpepers Herbal. New York: Sterling Publishing, 1983.

Rhode, Eleanour S. *Old English Herbals*. New York: Dover Publications, 1977.

Robers, Annie Lise. *Cornucopia*. New York: Knickerbocker Press, 1998.

Schapira, David. *Book of Coffee and Tea*. New York: St. Martin's Press, 1906.

Seymour, E.L.D. (BSA ED.) *Garden Encyclopedia*. New York: W.M. Hwise & Co., 1936.

Singer, C. *From Magic to Science*. New York: Dover Publications, 1928.

Standard Dictionary of Folklore, Mythology, and Legend. San Francisco: Harper San Francisco, 1984.

Telesco, Patricia. *Herbal Arts*. Secaucus, N.J.: Citadel Press, 1998.

———. *Victorian Flower Oracle*. St. Paul, Minn.: Llewellyn Publications, 1994.

Walker, Barbara. *Woman's Dictionary of Symbols and Sacred Objects*. New York: Harper & Row, 1988.

Wasserman, James. *Art & Symbols of the Occult*. Rochester, Vt.: Destiny Books, 1993.

Index

About the Author

Patricia Telesco is a mother of three, wife, chief human to five pets, and full-time author with more than 50 metaphysical books on the market. These include *Goddess in My Pocket, Futuretelling, The Herbal Arts, The Kitchen Witch's Cookbook, Little Book of Love Magic, Your Book of Shadows, Spinning Spells: Weaving Wonders,* and other diverse titles, each of which represents a different area of spiritual interest for her and her readers.

Trish maintains a strong presence in metaphysical journals, including *Circle Network News* and *Silver Chalice,* and on the Internet through such popular sites as *www.witchvox.com* (festival focus) and her Web site at *www.loresinger.com.*

Trish considers herself a down-to-earth, militant, wooden spoon–wielding Kitchen Witch whose love of folklore and worldwide customs flavor every energy and spell.